GUITAR CHORDS, Scales & Arpeggios

The Complete Guitar Reference Book

I0088635

Guitar Command

www.GuitarCommand.com

By Laurence Harwood.

Edited by Dan Wright.

Published by Timescale Music

ISBN: 978-0-9556566-6-8

Contents

Introduction

Guitar Chords, Scales And Arpeggios contains a large amount of information presented in a clear visual format. You can work through the book from beginning to end, or use it to find specific chords, scales or arpeggios whenever you need them.

This book is suitable for electric and acoustic guitarists of all styles and abilities. Use it to learn: basic chords to play and write new songs; barre chords for rock, pop and metal; complex jazz chords for creative comping; and scales and arpeggios for improvising guitar solos. Having a good knowledge of chords, scales and arpeggios is extremely beneficial whatever kind of music you play.

Much of the information in this book is presented in diagram form; you do not have to read music to use the book.

Notation and tab have been provided in addition to fretboard diagrams in the scales and arpeggios sections. The scales and arpeggios are notated with a root note of C. This allows guitarists to compare how the fretboard diagrams relate to the actual musical notation.

In many sections of the book, movable shapes for chords, scales and arpeggios have been provided. This means that, using just one shape, a chord, scale or arpeggio can be played with any root note.

Multiple shapes are provided for all of the movable chords and scales. This allows chords to be played in several positions and scales to be extended over the whole of the fretboard.

We hope that you enjoy using this book and that your playing benefits from the information it contains.

. . . .

Guitar Command

Guitar Command is a website and specialist guitar publisher.

Visit **www.GuitarCommand.com** for guitar news, information and free lessons. Improve your lead guitar playing with **Guitar Command Backing Track** albums, available to download from online stores.

Guitar Chords

This part of the book contains a comprehensive collection of guitar chords for use in all styles of music. It is arranged in three sections:

1. Basic Guitar Chords

This section contains a selection of open-position chords. These are relatively easy to play and should be among the first chords a beginner guitarist learns.

2. Guitar Chords Quick Reference

Use this section to find the chord you need quickly and easily. Diagrams of all of the common types of chord are included with every root note. Alternative ways of playing each type of chord are provided in the Movable Chord Shapes section.

3. Movable Chord Shapes

This section contains movable shapes for a large number of chords. Movable chord shapes can be moved up and down the fretboard in order to play the same type of chord (e.g. major, minor, etc.) with a different root note.

How To Read Chord Diagrams

Guitar chord diagrams represent the guitar fretboard. They show where the fretting fingers should be placed in order to play a chord.

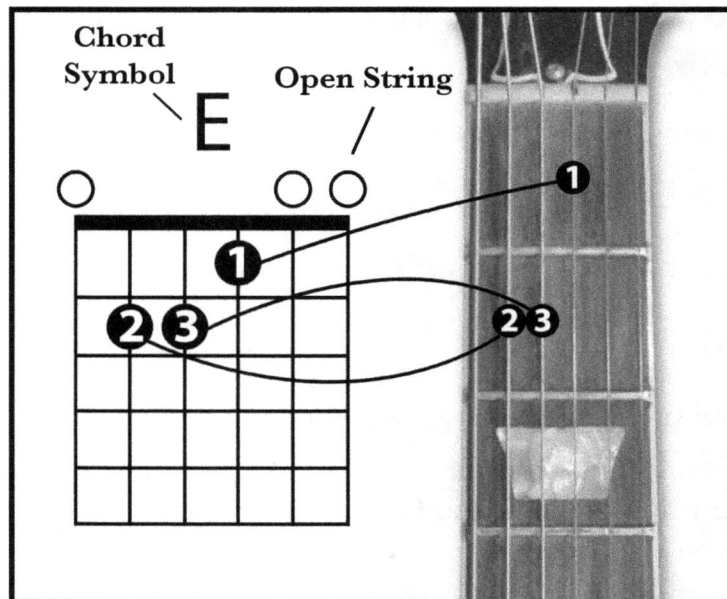

How A Chord Diagram Relates To The Guitar Neck

Standard Fretting Finger Numbering

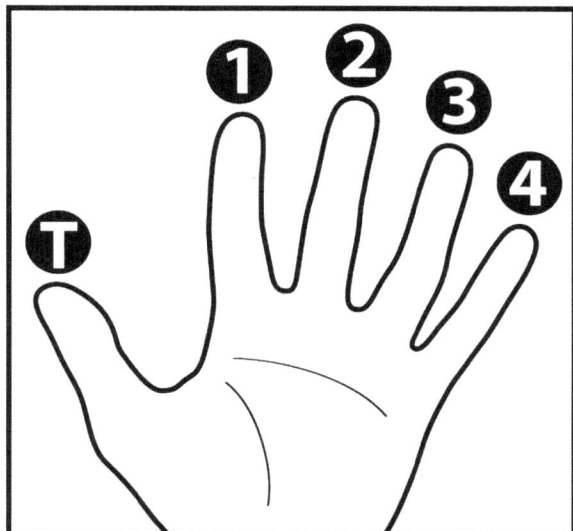

1: Index Finger

2: Middle Finger

3: Ring Finger

4: Little Finger

T: Thumb

The chord fingerings in this book are provided as suggestions only; feel free to experiment with your own.

Information About Chord Diagrams

The vertical lines in a chord diagram represent the guitar strings, with the bottom E string on the left. The horizontal lines are the frets.

The black circles show where the fingers should be placed; the numbers inside these circles show which fingers should be used.

A circle or 'O' above a string shows that the string is played as part of the chord but is not fingered, i.e. it is left 'open'.

An 'X' above a string means that the string should not be played. Avoid hitting it with your plectrum or fingers when you strum the chord, or stop it from ringing with another fretting finger.

A thicker horizontal line on the top of some chord diagrams represents the 'nut' of the guitar. The nut is the grooved ridge that separates the fretboard and the headstock. Position your fingers in relation to the nut.

For diagrams without a nut, a number to the side shows at which fret the chord should be played.

A diagram showing all of the notes on a guitar fretboard is provided on page 9. Refer to this diagram when you need to know where to position a movable chord shape. See the 'Movable Chords' section for more information.

Root Notes

An 'R' next to a note in a movable chord shape diagram shows the **root note** of the chord. The root note of a chord is the note that gives the chord its name, i.e. the 'C' of C major, or the 'G' of G minor 9th.

Tips For Playing Guitar Chords

- *Experiment with where you put your fingers in the frets. Positioning fingers closer to the fretwire (towards the right of the fret on a standard, right-handed guitar) can minimise fretbuzz and make chords easier to play.*

- *When you are learning a chord, try playing the notes one at a time rather than all at once. This will let you know if every note in the chord is sounding correctly. If any notes sound dull or are not sounding at all, shuffle your fingers around until all of the notes ring out clearly.*

- *Remember, if you are having problems getting all of the notes to sound, it is usually a case of moving your fingers around to find a more efficient position rather than simply pressing down harder.*

- *Learning just one movable chord shape means that you can play that chord with any root note. Therefore, if you learn a movable major chord shape, you can play any major chord!*

- *However, to avoid either playing chords too high up the fretboard or having to jump around the fretboard too much, it is always useful to know more than one way of playing each type of chord.*

Which Chord Shape To Use?

Most types of chord can be played in several different ways. For example, a C major chord can be played in open position or further up the fretboard as a movable chord.

Printed music often specifies only the *type* of chord to be played rather than the actual chord shape to be used. It is left up to the guitarist to decide how to play the chord.

Open position chords can sound brighter and are often easier to play than barre chords, particularly on acoustic guitars. However, they are not as easy to dampen for complex rhythmic patterns and their sound can be overbearing in some situations.

Barre chords and other movable shapes are more versatile but can sound less 'full' and can be harder to move to and from smoothly.

There are no hard and fast rules for selecting which chord shape to use. Your choice will depend on the style of music, the strumming pattern you are using, the tempo of the song and the sound of the chord. The best advice as always is to let your ears be the judge.

Guitar Fretboard Diagram

Use the guitar fretboard diagram below to position movable chord shapes. Standard string numbering is used, from 6 (the low E string) to 1 (the high E string).

The shaded areas on the diagram represent the frets which, on most guitars, contain dots or other inlaid markers.

String

Fret Number	6	5	4	3	2	1
Open	E	A	D	G	B	E
1	F	A#/Bb	D#/Eb	G#/Ab	C	F
2	F#/Gb	B	E	A	C#/Db	F#/Gb
3	G	C	F	A#/Bb	D	G
4	G#/Ab	C#/Db	F#/Gb	B	D#/Eb	G#/Ab
5	A	D	G	C	E	A
6	A#/Bb	D#/Eb	G#/Ab	C#/Db	F	A#/Bb
7	B	E	A	D	F#/Gb	B
8	C	F	A#/Bb	D#/Eb	G	C
9	C#/Db	F#/Gb	B	E	G#/Ab	C#/Db
10	D	G	C	F	A	D
11	D#/Eb	G#/Ab	C#/Db	F#/Gb	A#/Bb	D#/Eb
12	E	A	D	G	B	E

(At the 12th fret, notes are repeated an octave higher.)

Basic Guitar Chords

These chords are among the first a guitarist should learn. However, they're not just for beginners – most guitarists will continue to use these chords throughout their careers.

Major Chords

E
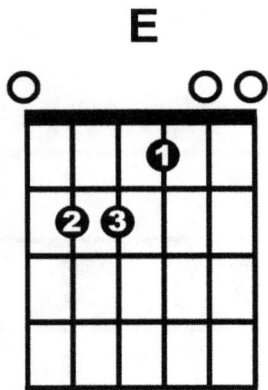

C
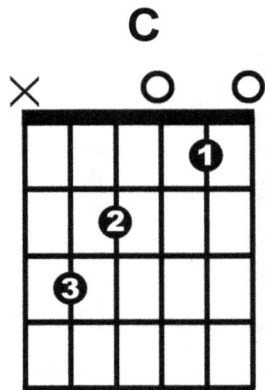

D
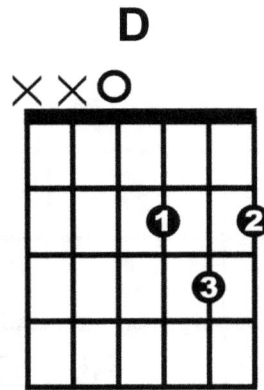

G
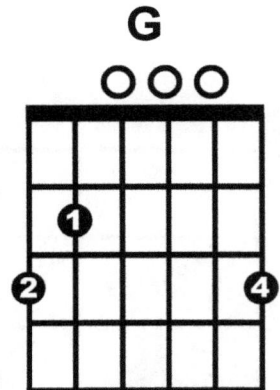

A
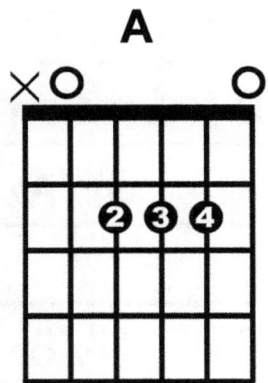

F
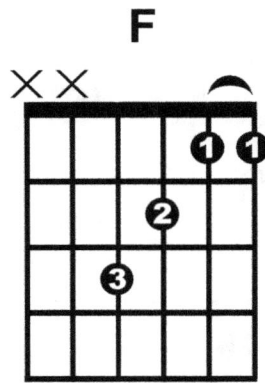

Minor Chords

Em
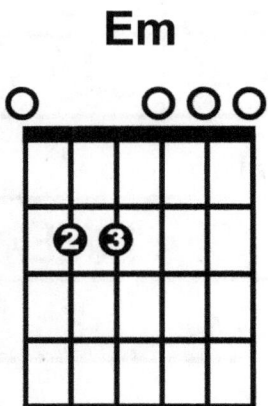

Am
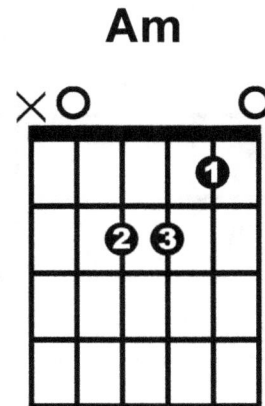

Dm
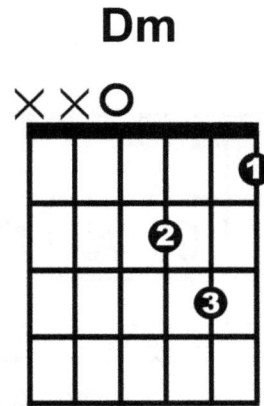

Dominant 7th Chords

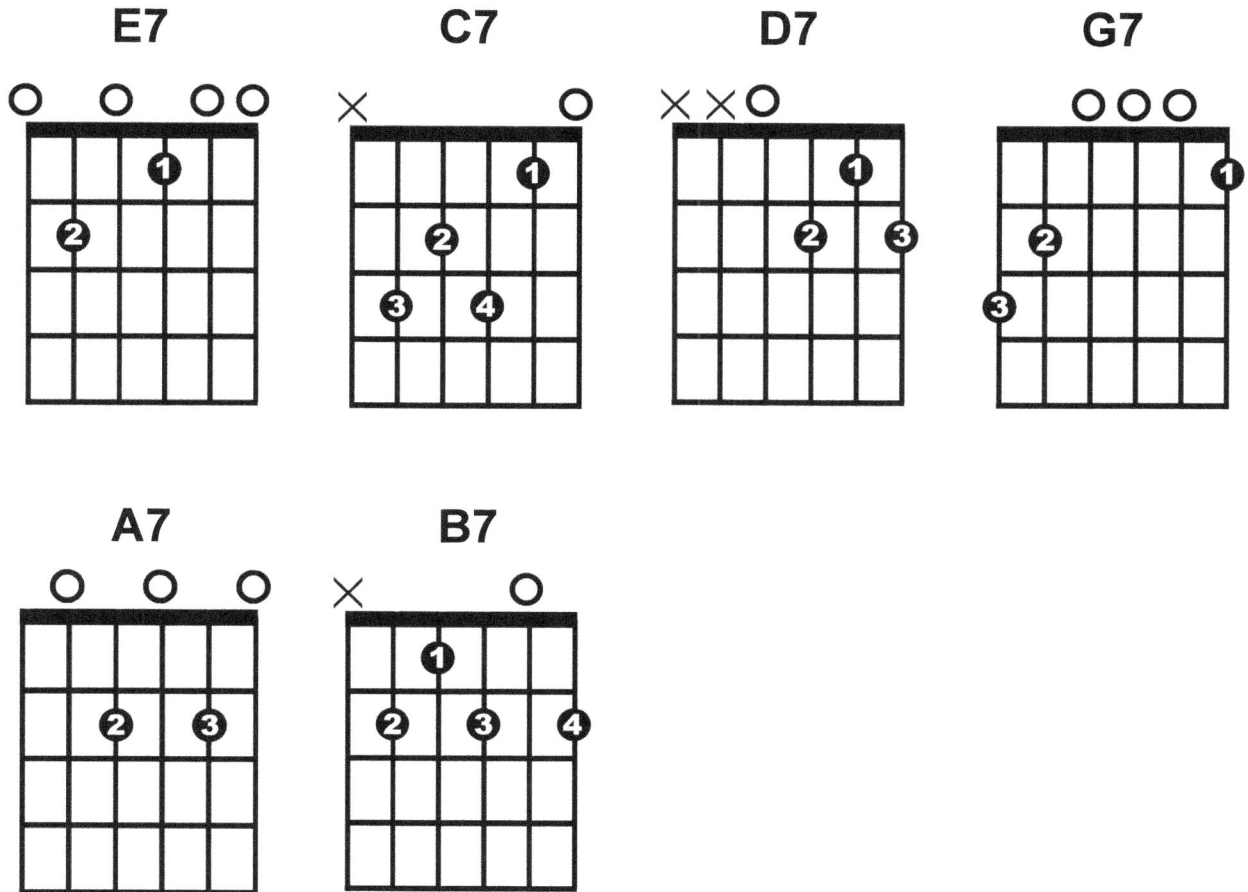

E7

C7

D7

G7

A7

B7

Guitar Chords - Quick Reference

This section contains all of the commonly used chord types with every root note. Open-position versions of the chords have been used wherever possible. For alternative versions of each chord, and for chord types not included here, refer to the 'Movable Chords' section.

Note: pairs of chords such as F sharp major and G flat major are 'enharmonically equivalent', i.e. they are the same chord despite having different names. In this chapter, both names have been given for enharmonically equivalent chords. They are not 'slash chords' (see the slash chords section).

Major Chords

E
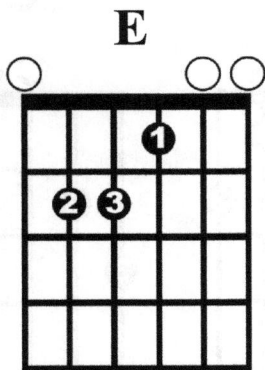

F
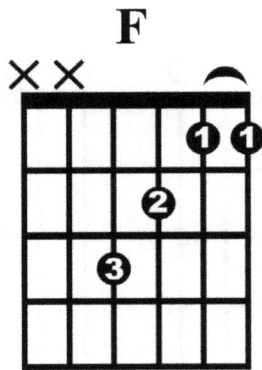

F♯ / G♭
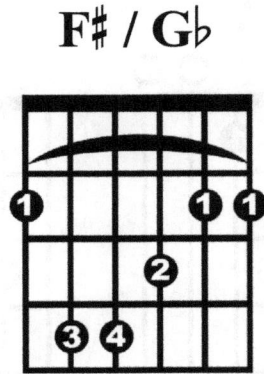

G
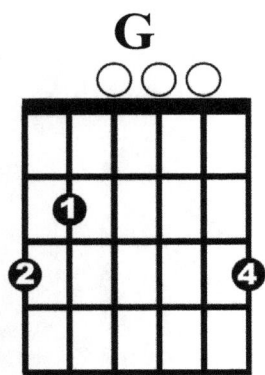

G♯ / A♭
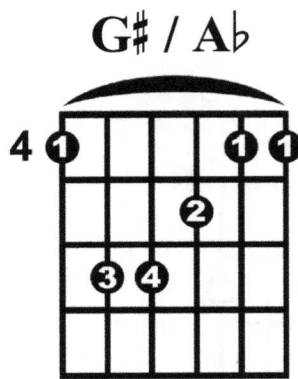

A
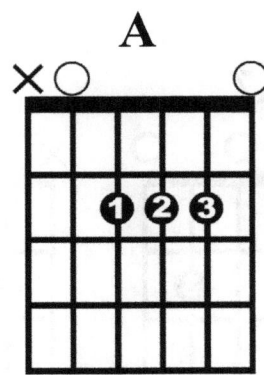

A♯ / B♭
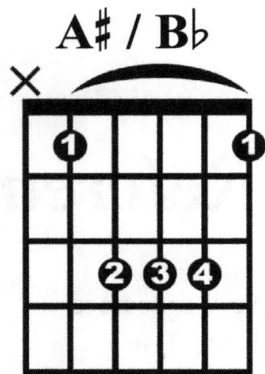

B
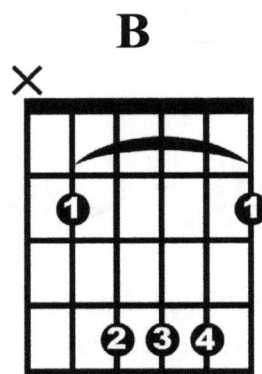

C
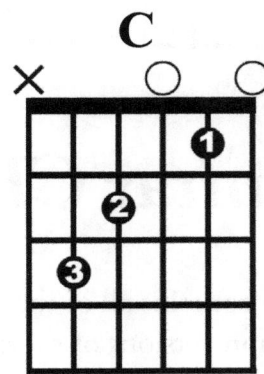

C♯ / D♭
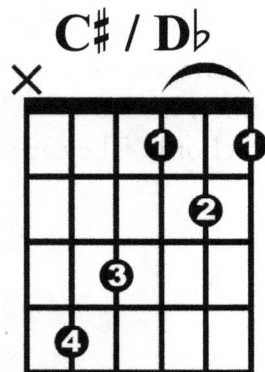

D
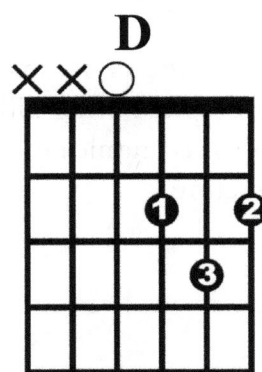

D♯ / E♭
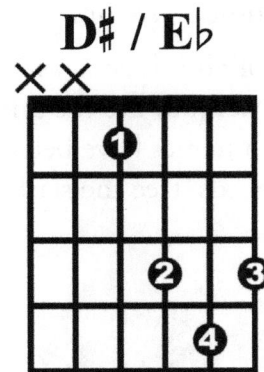

Minor (m) Chords

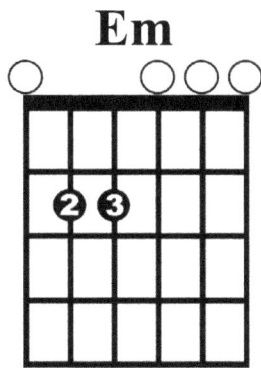

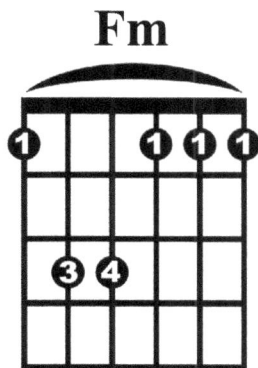

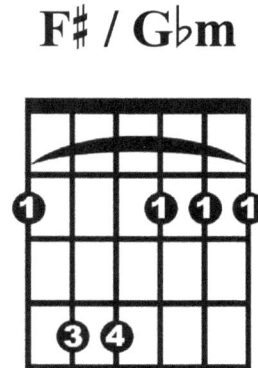

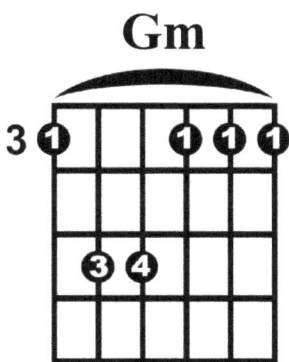

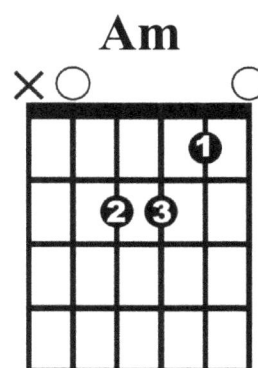

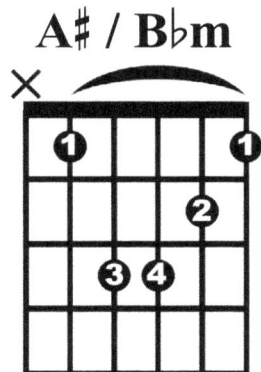

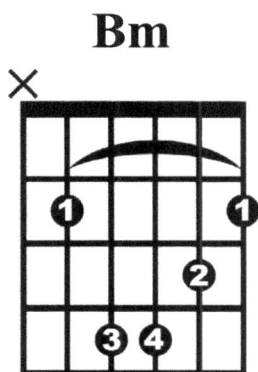

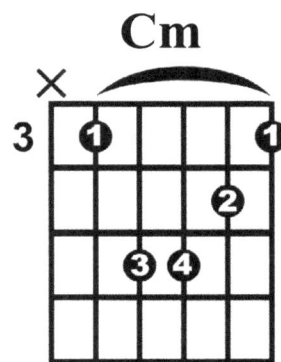

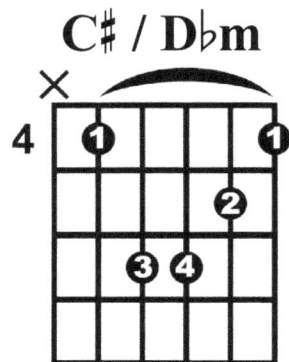

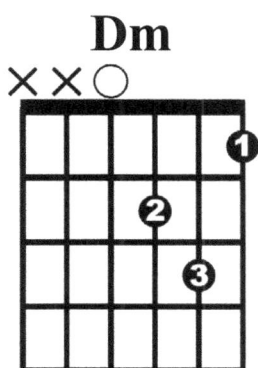

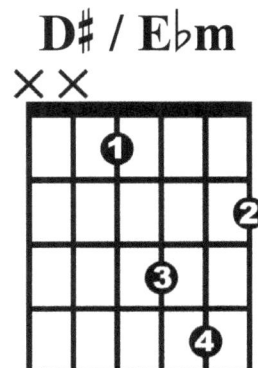

Dominant 7th (7) Chords

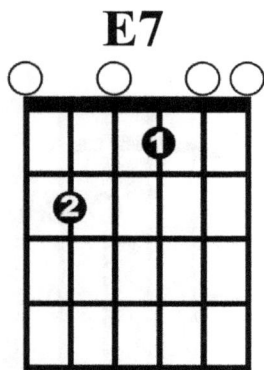

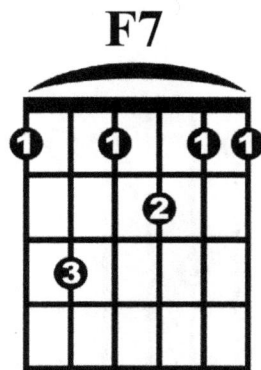

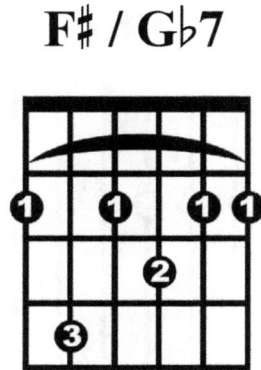

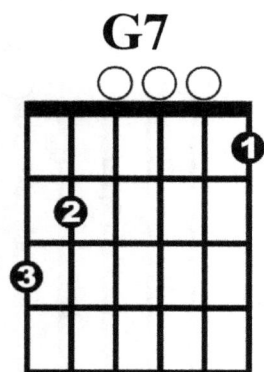

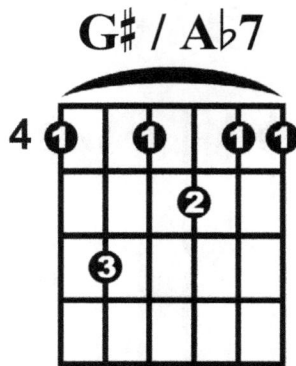

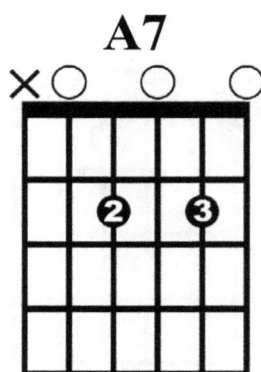

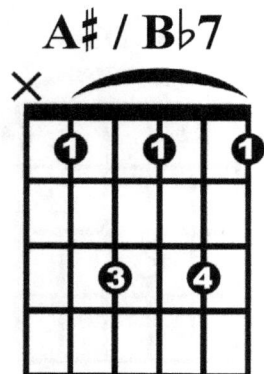

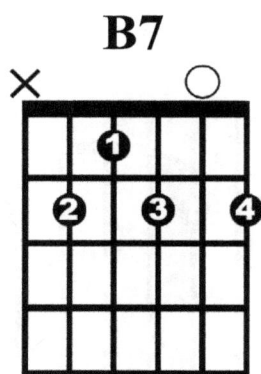

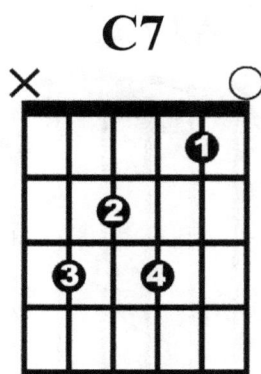

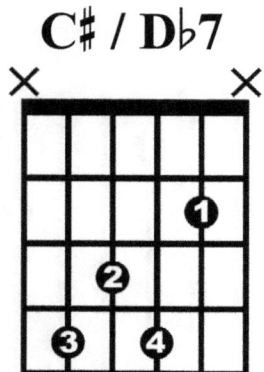

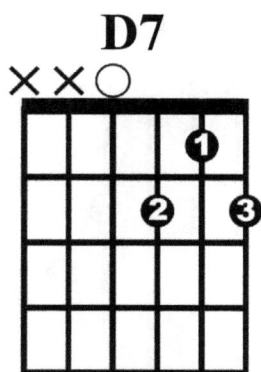

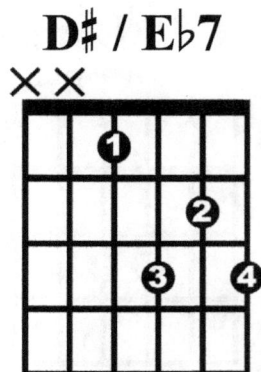

14

Minor 7th (m7) Chords

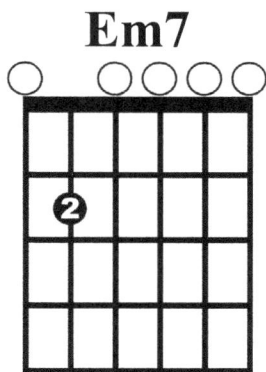

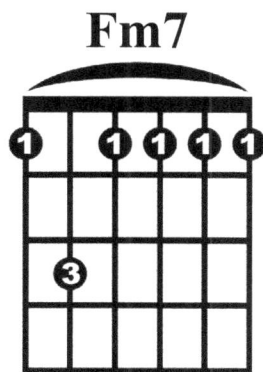

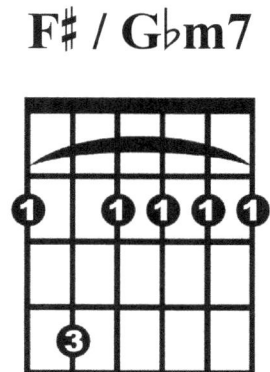

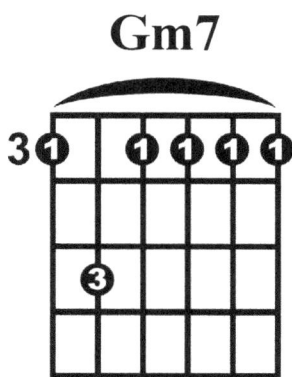

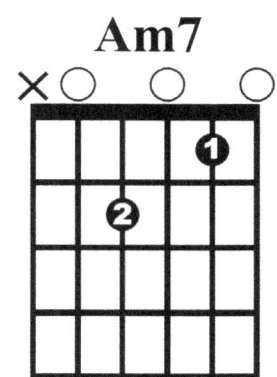

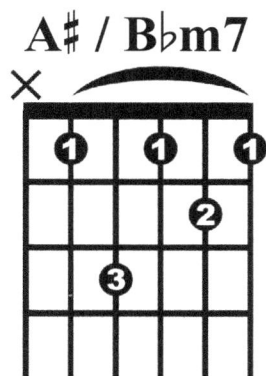

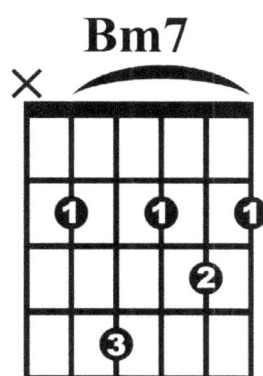

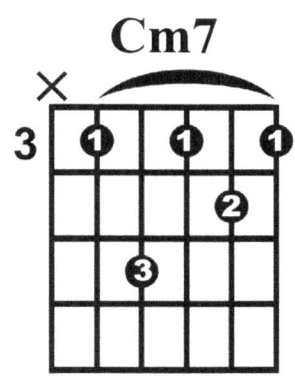

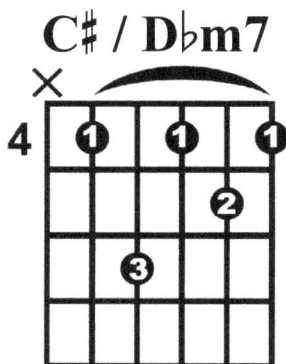

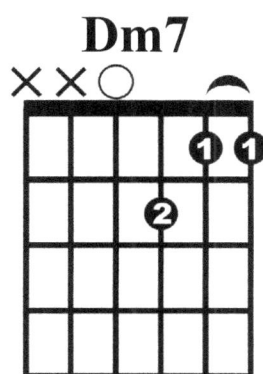

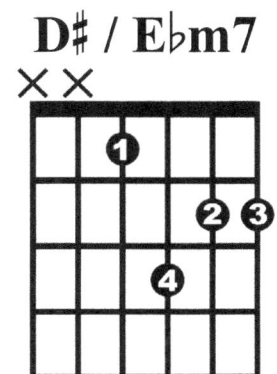

Em7

Fm7

F♯ / G♭m7

Gm7

G♯ / A♭m7

Am7

A♯ / B♭m7

Bm7

Cm7

C♯ / D♭m7

Dm7

D♯ / E♭m7

Major 7th (maj7) Chords

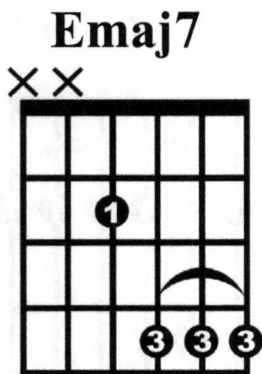

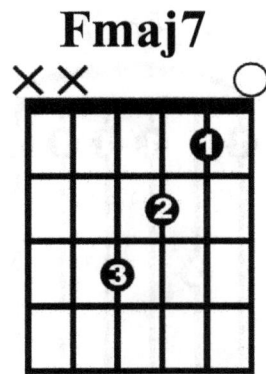

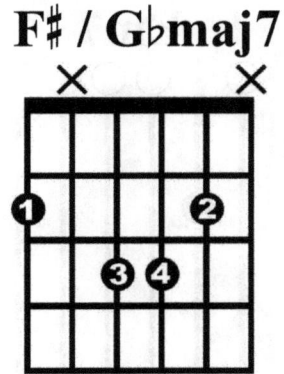

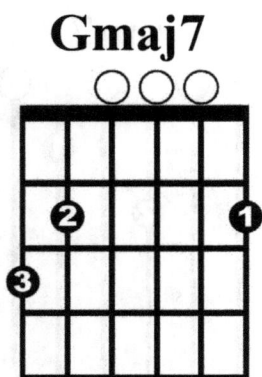

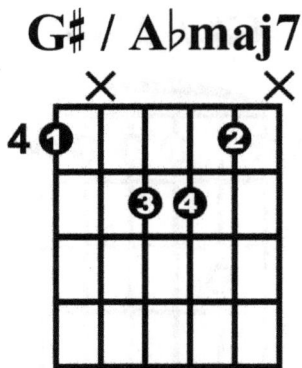

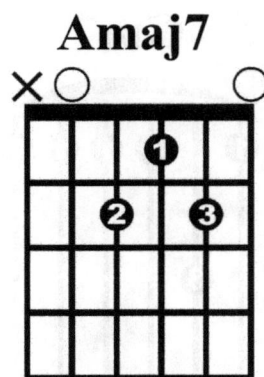

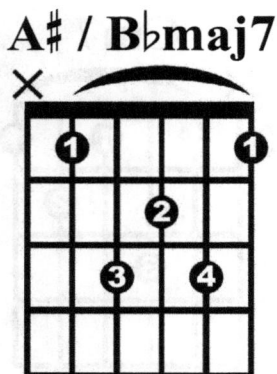

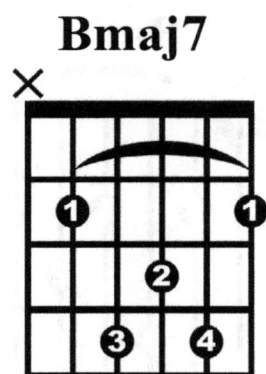

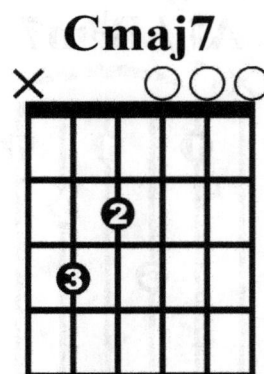

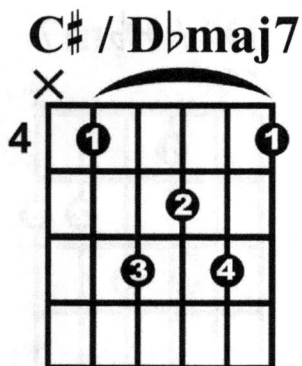

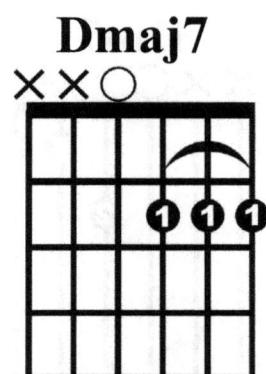

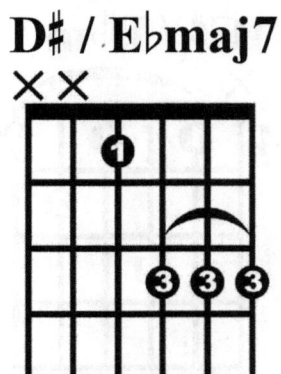

Emaj7

Fmaj7

F# / Gbmaj7

Gmaj7

G# / Abmaj7

Amaj7

A# / Bbmaj7

Bmaj7

Cmaj7

C# / Dbmaj7

Dmaj7

D# / Ebmaj7

Major 6th (6) Chords

Minor 6th (m6) Chords

Em6
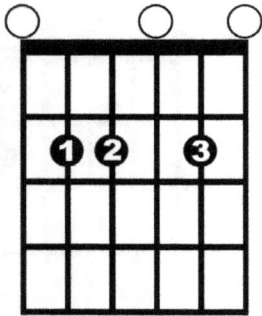

Fm6
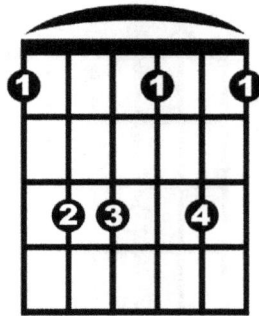

F# / G♭m6
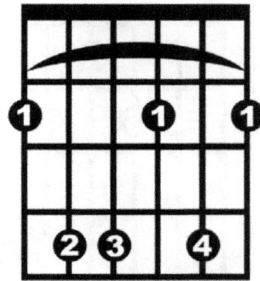

Gm6
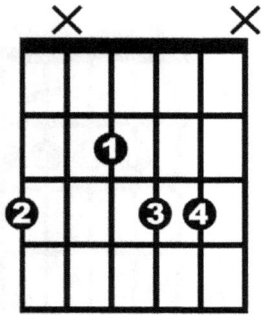

G# / A♭m6
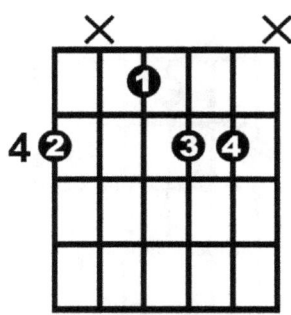

Am6
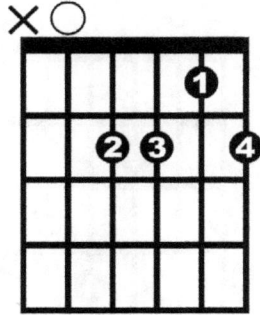

A# / B♭m6
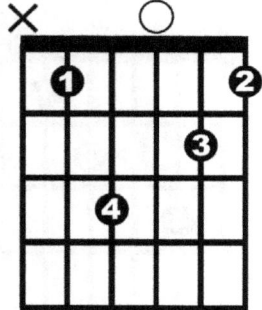

Bm6
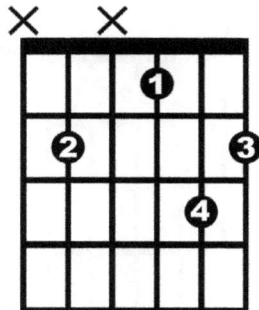

Cm6
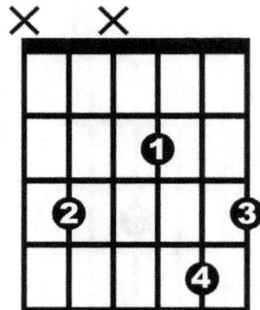

C# / D♭m6
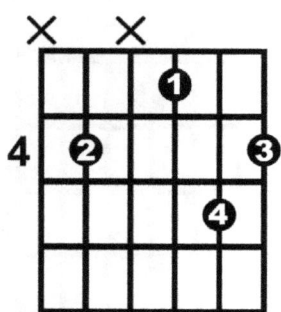

Dm6
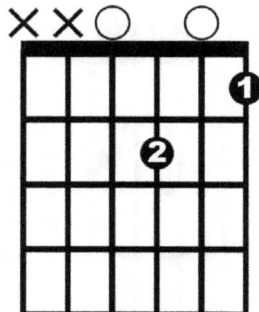

D# / E♭m6
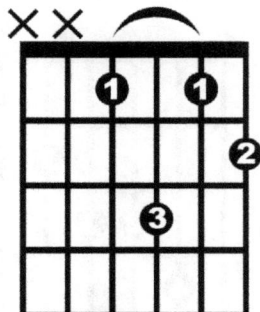

Diminished 7th (dim7 or °7) Chords

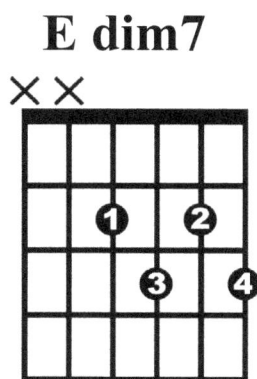

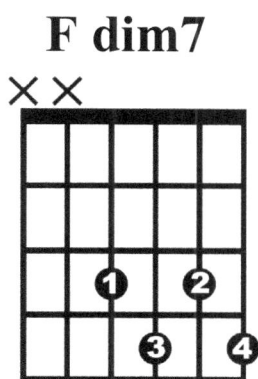

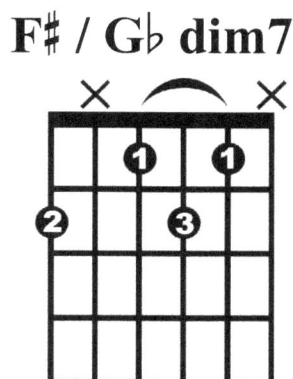

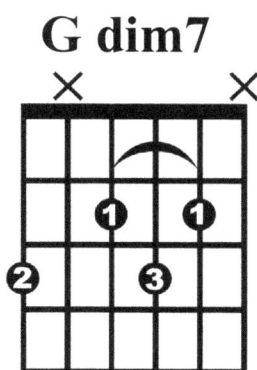

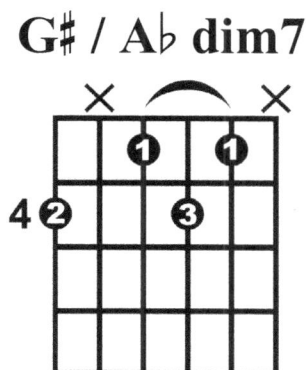

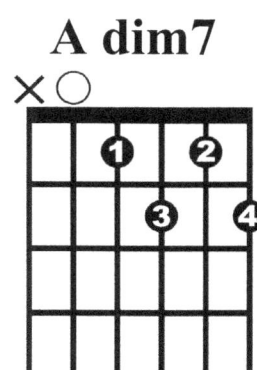

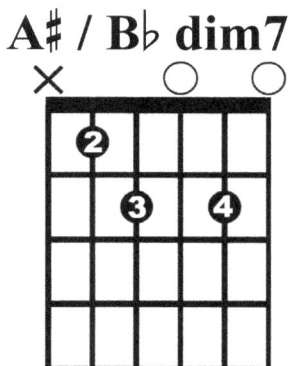

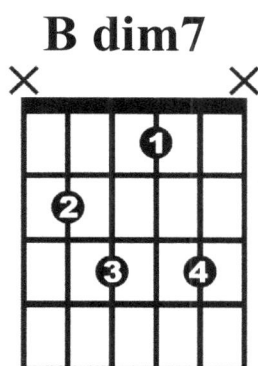

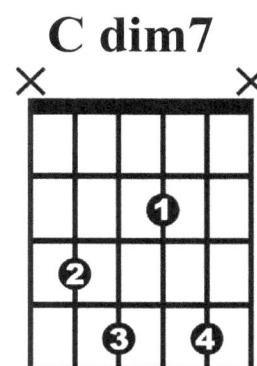

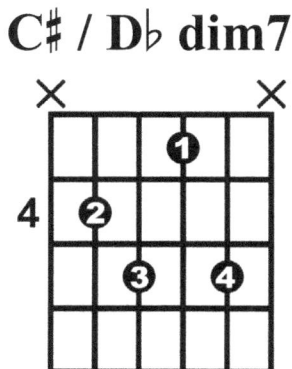

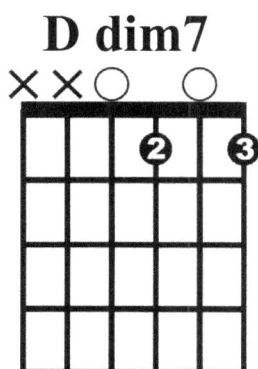

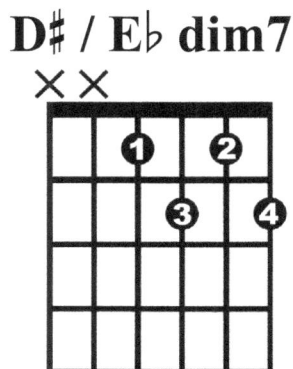

E dim7

F dim7

F♯ / G♭ dim7

G dim7

G♯ / A♭ dim7

A dim7

A♯ / B♭ dim7

B dim7

C dim7

C♯ / D♭ dim7

D dim7

D♯ / E♭ dim7

Dominant 9th (9) Chords

20

Suspended 4th (sus4) Chords

E sus4
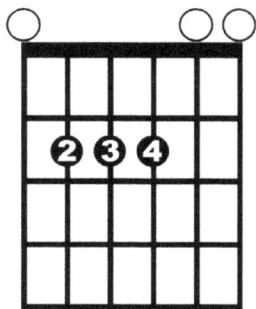

F sus4
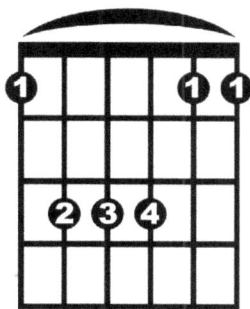

F♯ / G♭ sus4
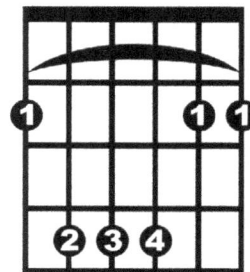

G sus4
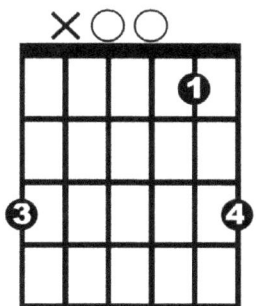

G♯ / A♭ sus4
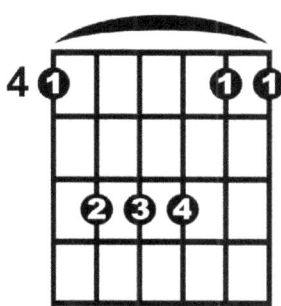

A sus4
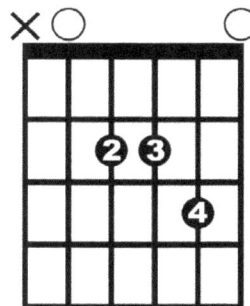

A♯ / B♭ sus4
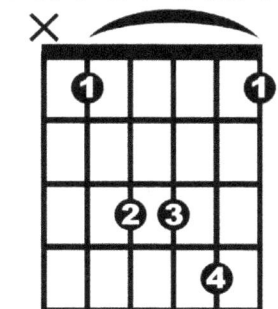

B sus4
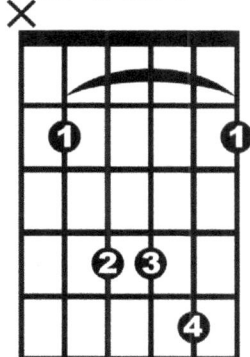

C sus4
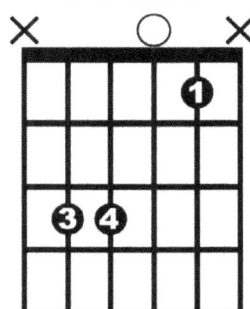

C♯ / D♭ sus4
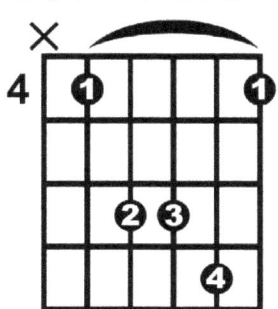

D sus4
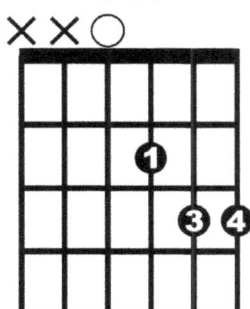

D♯ / E♭ sus4
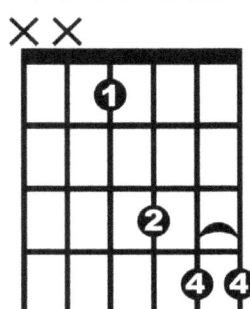

Suspended 2nd (sus2) Chords

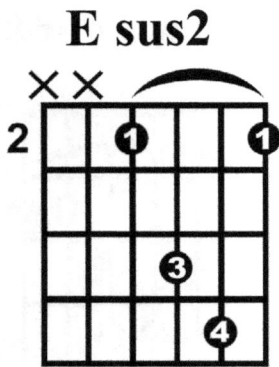

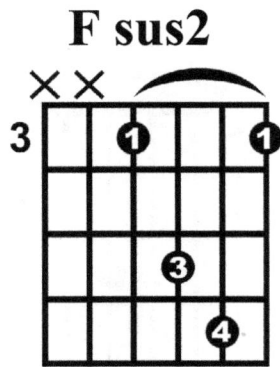

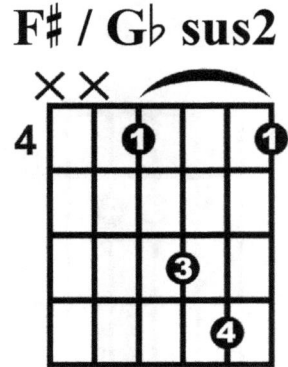

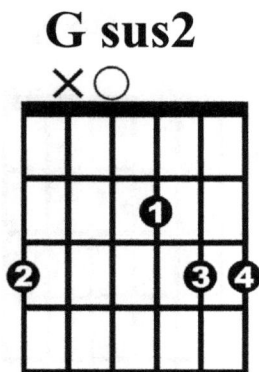

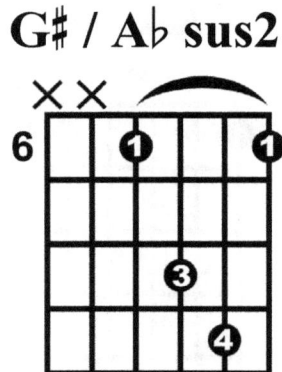

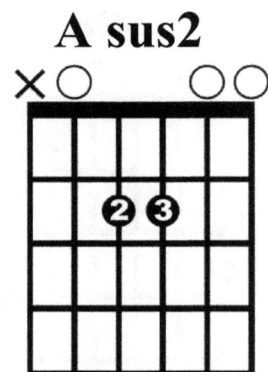

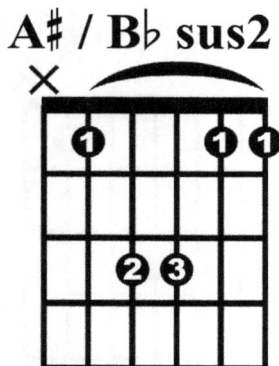

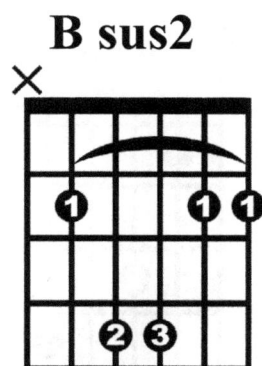

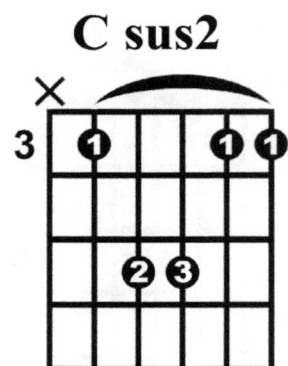

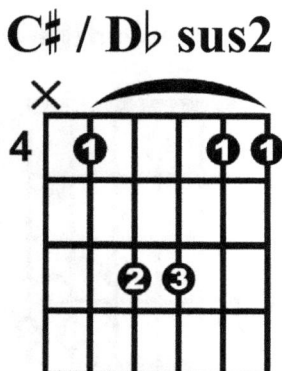

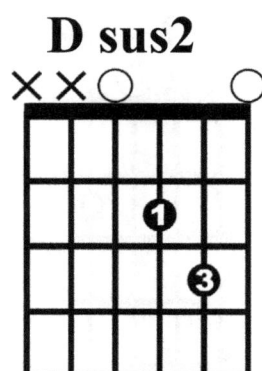

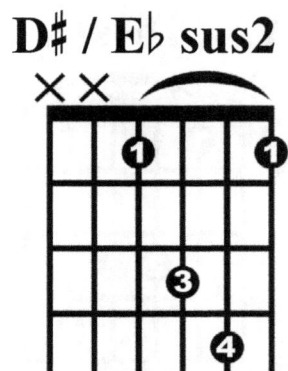

E sus2

F sus2

F# / G♭ sus2

G sus2

G# / A♭ sus2

A sus2

A# / B♭ sus2

B sus2

C sus2

C# / D♭ sus2

D sus2

D# / E♭ sus2

Major Add Nine (add 9) Chords

E add9
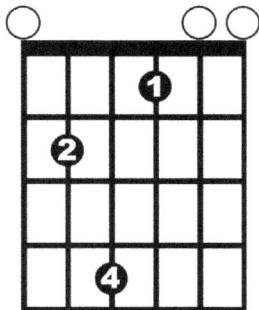

F add9
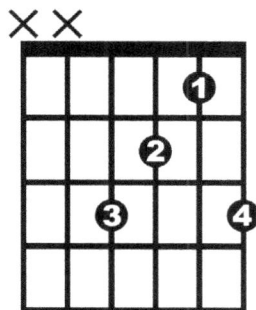

F♯ / G♭ add9
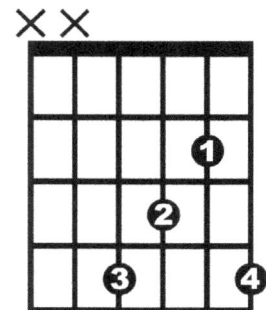

G add9
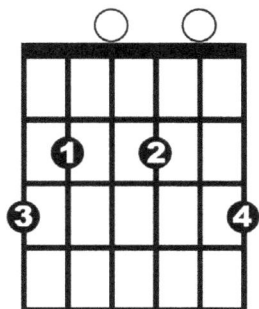

G♯ / A♭ add9
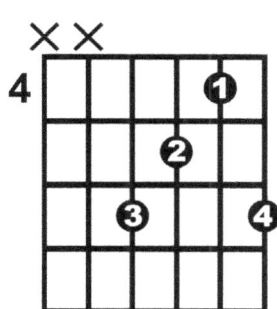

A add9
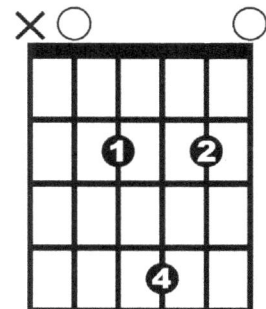

A♯ / B♭ add9
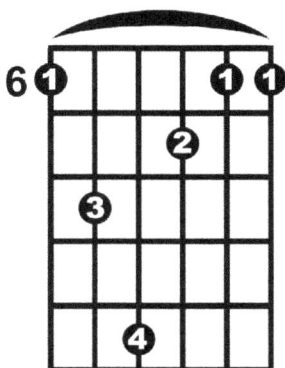

B add9
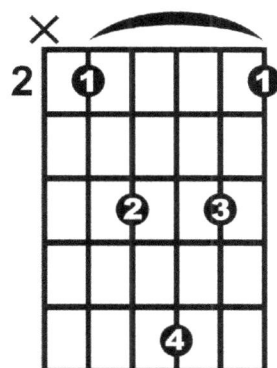

C add9
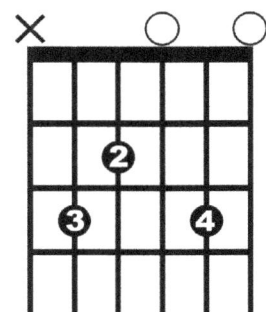

C♯ / D♭ add9
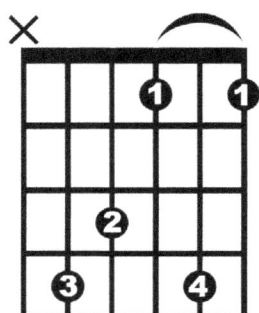

D add9
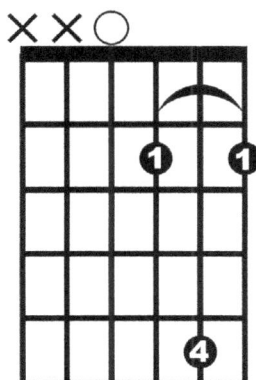

D♯ / E♭ add9
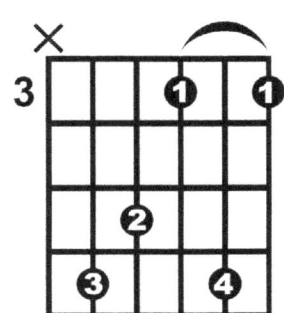

Minor Add Nine (m add9) Chords

Em add9
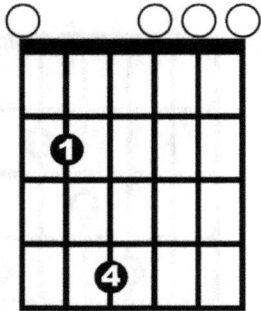

Fm add9
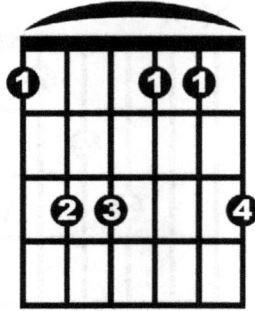

F# / G♭m add9
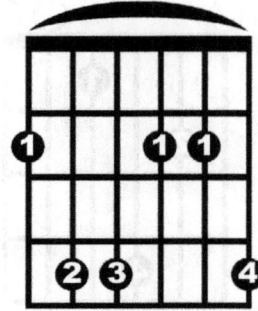

Gm add9
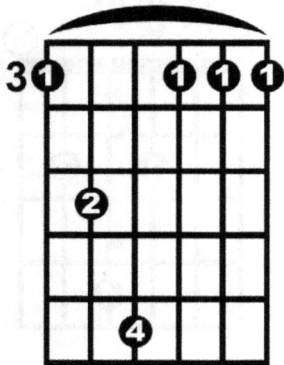

G# / A♭m add9
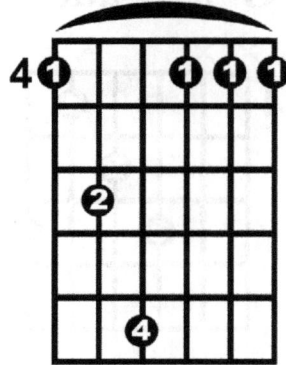

Am add9
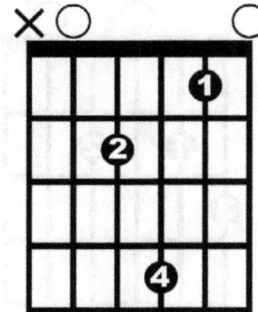

A# / B♭m add9
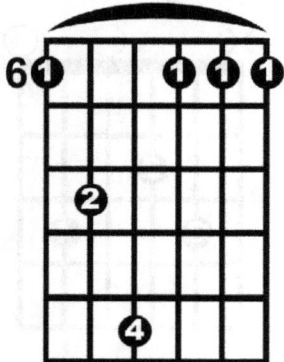

Bm add9
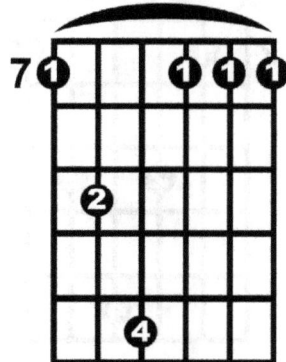

Cm add9
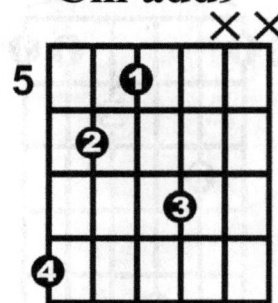

C# / D♭m add9
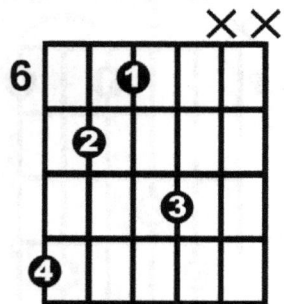

Dm add9
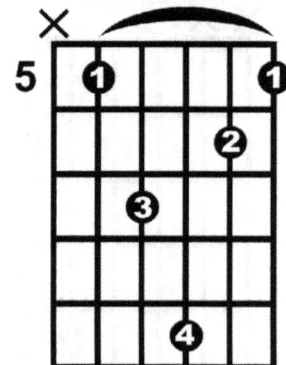

D# / E♭m add9
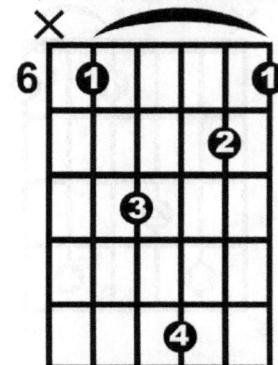

Power Chords (5)

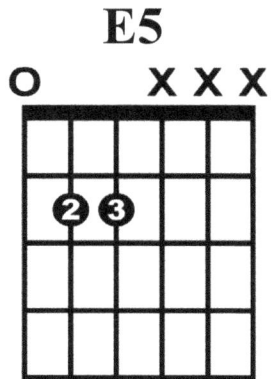

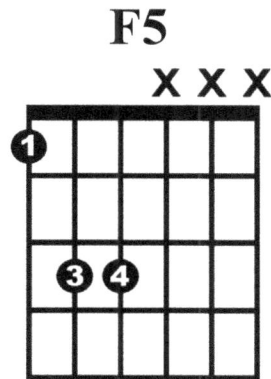

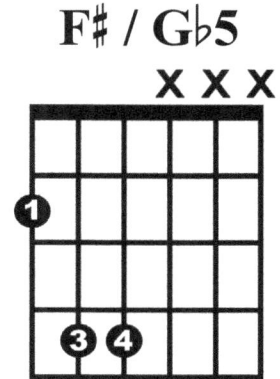

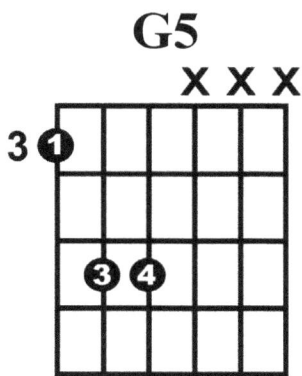

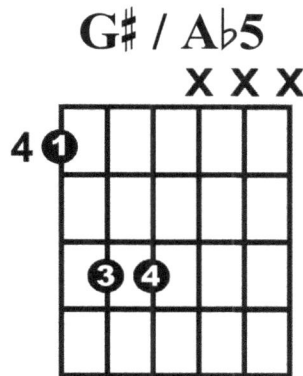

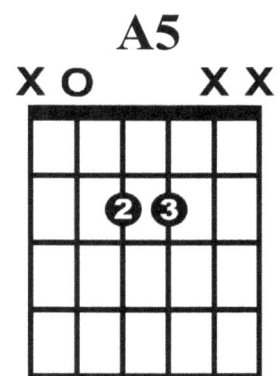

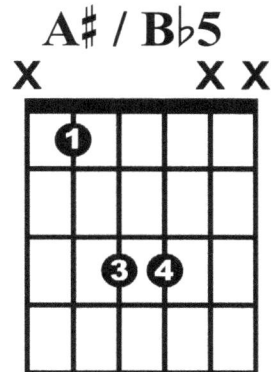

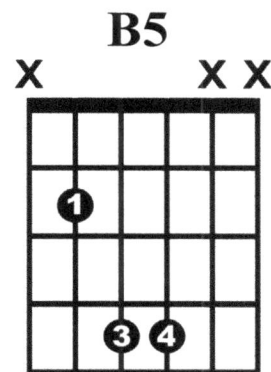

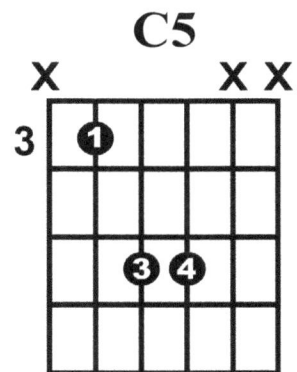

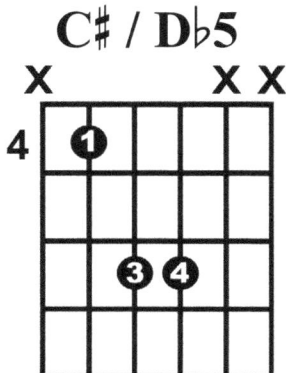

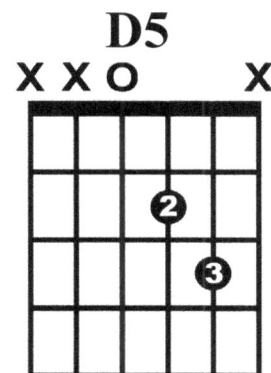

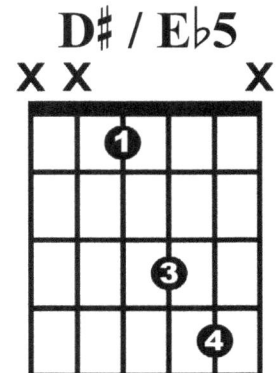

Slash Chords

Slash chord symbols specify both the chord itself, and a bass note that should be added to the chord. For example, a D/F♯ slash chord is a D major chord with an F sharp as the lowest note. An Am/E chord is an A minor chord with an E in the bass.

Slash chords can be any chord with any bass note. Consult the fretboard diagram on page 9 if you are unsure where to play the slash note. Some common slash chords are shown below.

D/F♯

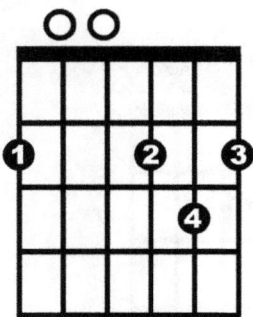

C/G

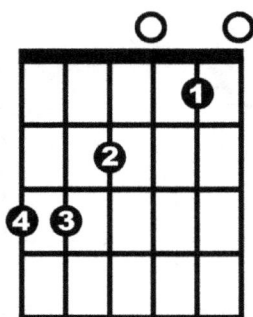

D/C

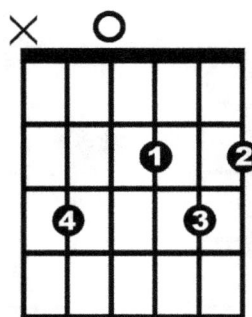

Am/G

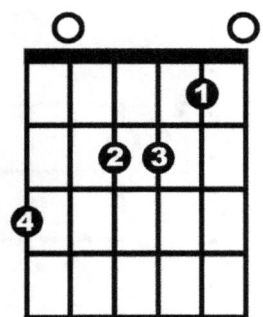

Movable Guitar Chords

The chords in this section of the book are all movable chord shapes. Movable chord shapes can be moved up and down the fretboard to make different chords. For example, the same movable major chord shape that produces a G major chord at the third fret will produce an A major chord if it is played two frets higher, at the fifth fret.

Many movable chord shapes require the use of a 'barre'. This is when a finger (usually the index finger) is placed across the fretboard and used to play more than one note at a time. Barres are represented by curved lines on chord diagrams.

Notes On Movable Chord Shapes

In all of the following diagrams, the root note of a chord shape is shown with an 'R'. Use the fretboard diagram on page 9 to find out where to position the chord shapes to play the desired chord.

In order to play some of the more complex chords on the guitar, notes occasionally have to be left out. This is because to play the whole chord would require either more guitar strings or more fingers than we actually have! The notes that are omitted are those that do not affect the overall nature of the chord. Occasionally, the root notes themselves are left out. Where this occurs, the position of the omitted root note is marked with an R in brackets: **(R)**. This allows the chord to be correctly positioned on the fretboard.

How To Use Movable Chord Shapes

To play a G major chord using the movable shape shown below, position the root note marked on the chord diagram over the G note on the 6th string.

Use the fretboard diagram on page 9 to locate the desired note if necessary.

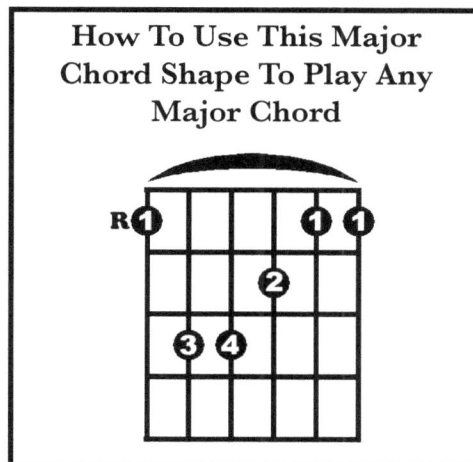

The root note of the chord shape is on the 6th string. There is a G at the third fret of the sixth string, therefore the shape should be played at the third fret for a G major chord.

The other fingers are positioned relative to the root note as shown in the diagram.

To play an A major chord using the same chord shape, the process is repeated, but this time the root note of the chord is positioned over an A note on the 6th string.

The A is two frets higher up the 6th string, at the fifth fret. Therefore, the whole chord shape is moved two frets higher to play an A major chord.

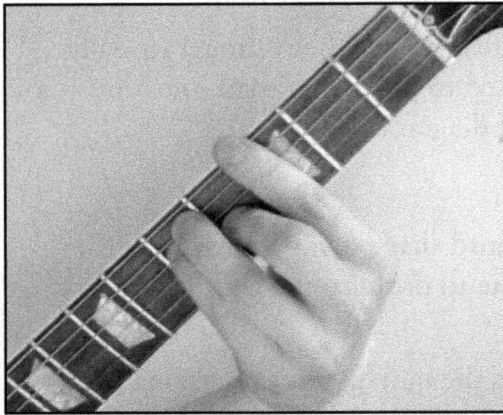

At the third fret, the major chord shape produces a G major chord.

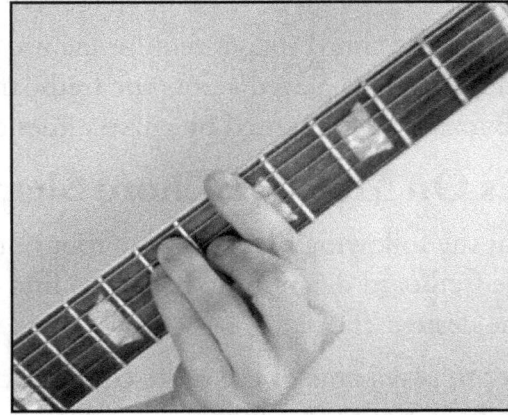

The same major chord shape, when played at the fifth fret, produces an A major chord.

The same shape can be used to play any major chord. For example, moving the same shape another two frets up the fretboard would produce a B major chord.

Major Chord Shapes

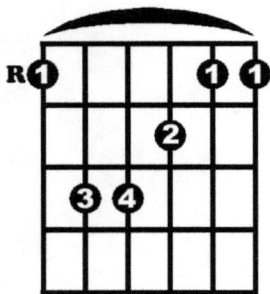

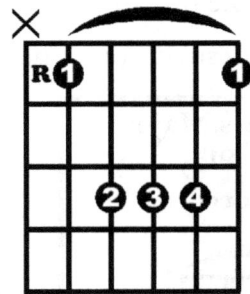

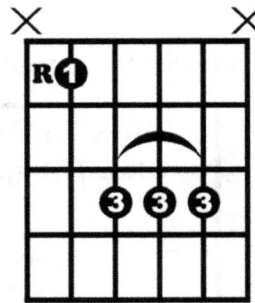

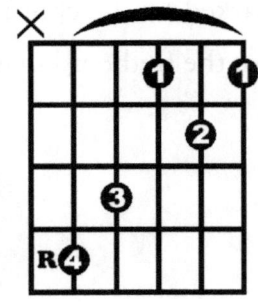

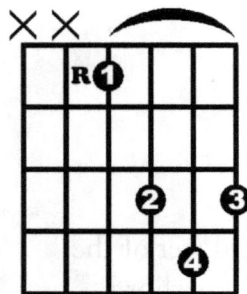

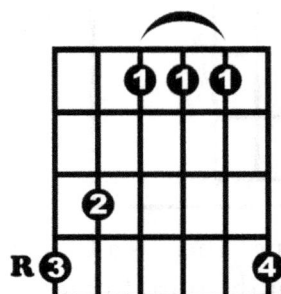

Minor (m) Chord Shapes

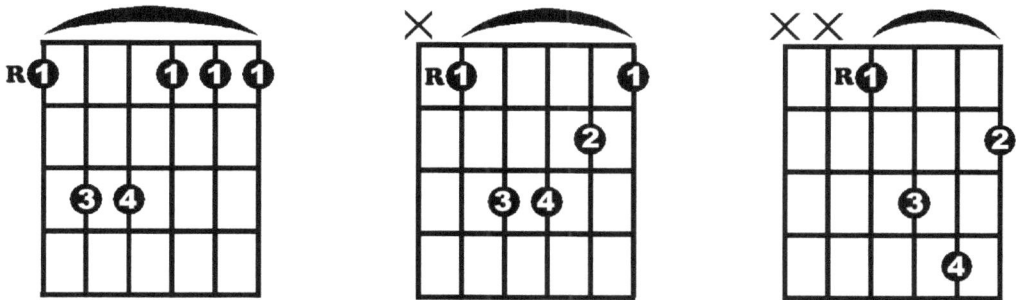

Dominant 7th (7) Chord Shapes

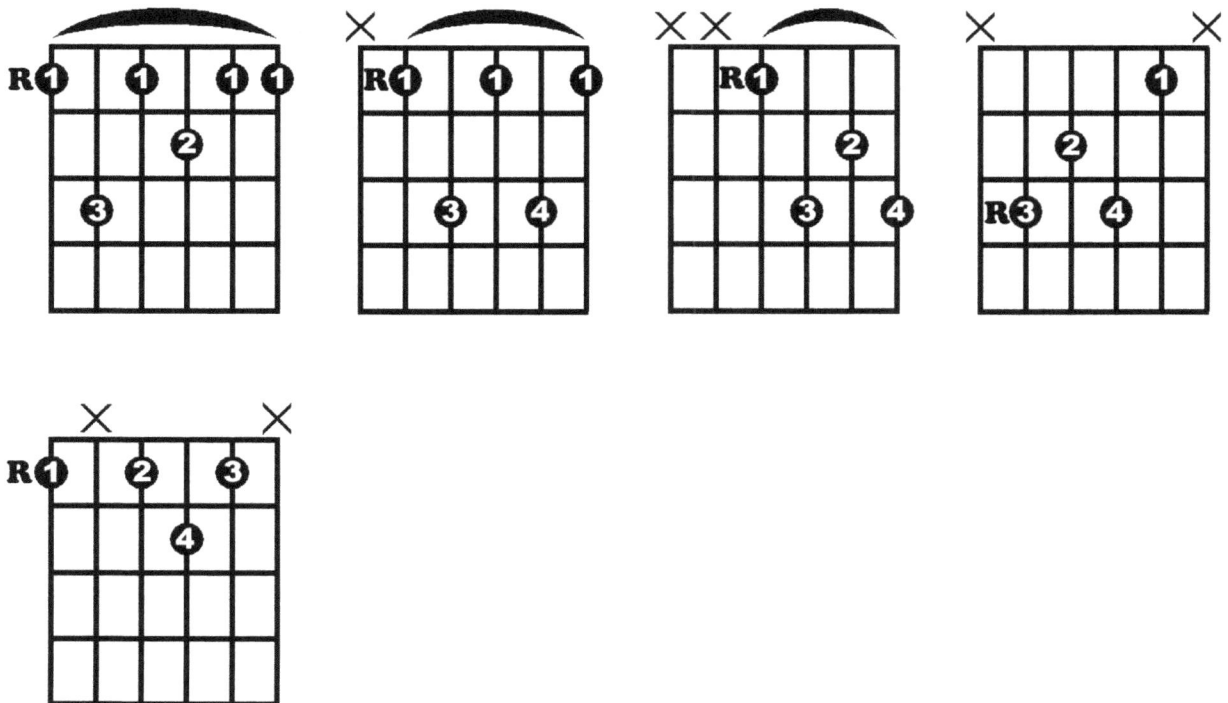

Minor 7th (m7) Chord Shapes

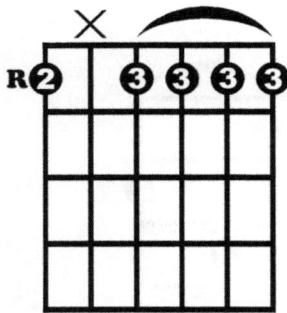

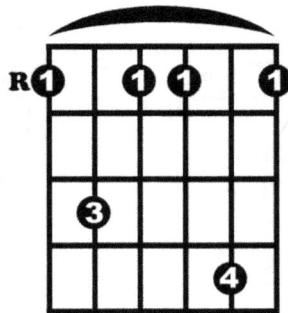

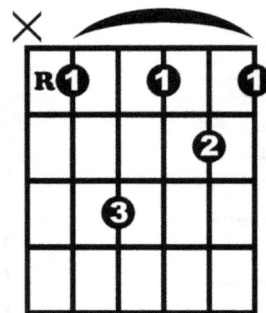

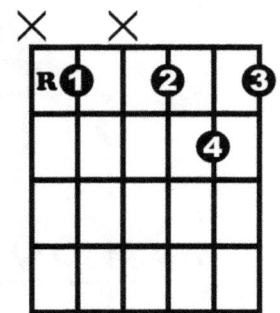

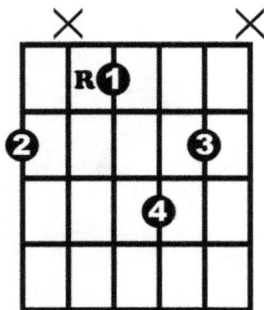

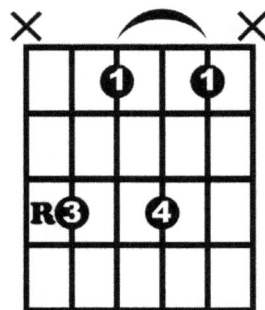

> Minor 7th chords can also be written with a dash '-' instead of an 'm', e.g. D-7

Power Chord (5) Chord Shapes

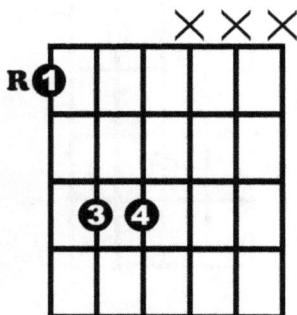

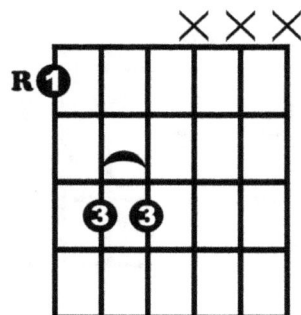

(Alternative Fingering)   (Alternative Fingering)

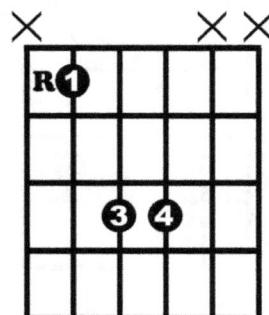

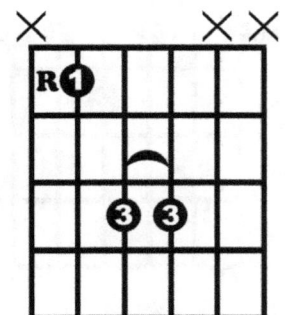

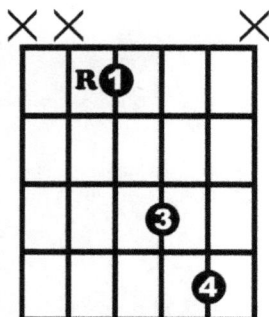

> As their name suggests, power chords have a powerful sound, ideal for use in rock and metal. Power chords are also known as fifth chords, as they contain only the root and fifth notes.

Suspended 4th (sus4) Chord Shapes

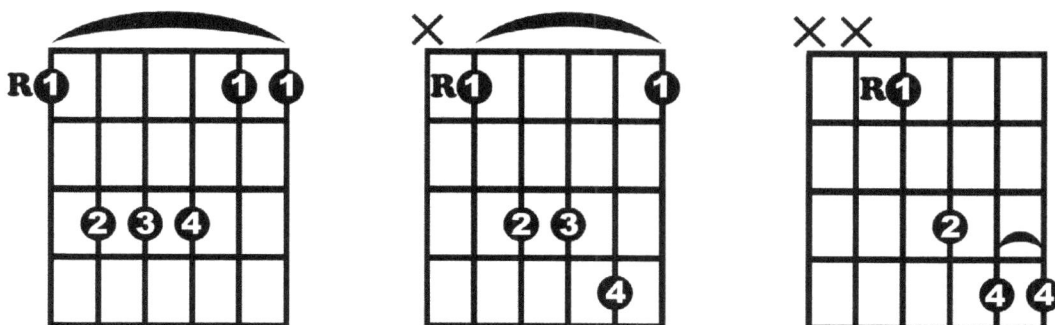

Suspended 2nd (sus2) Chord Shapes

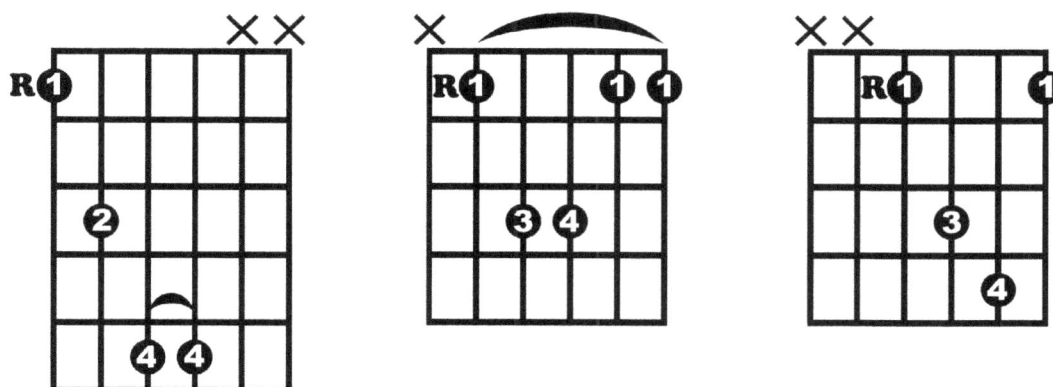

Dominant 7th Suspended 4th (7sus4) Chord Shapes

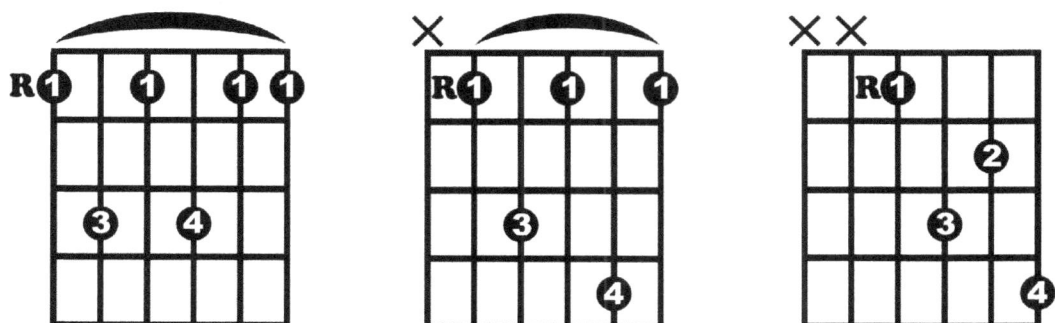

Major 7th (maj7) Chord Shapes

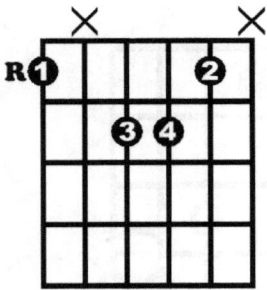

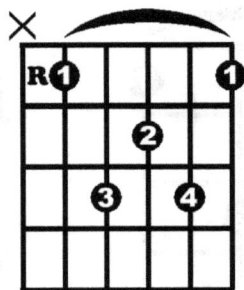

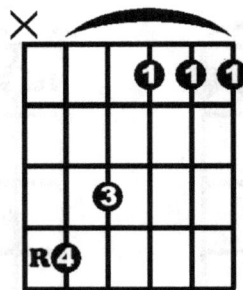

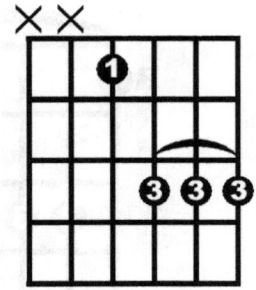

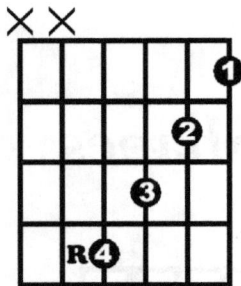

Another commonly used symbol for a major seventh chord is a triangle: Δ

Major 6th (6) Chord Shapes

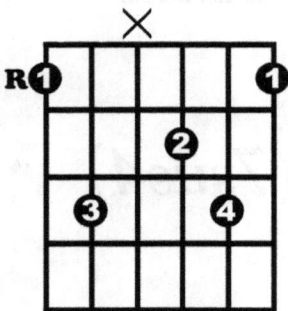

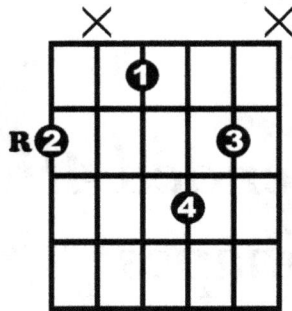

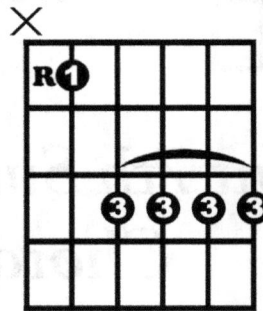

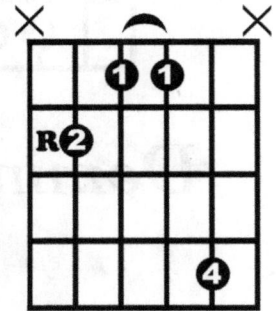

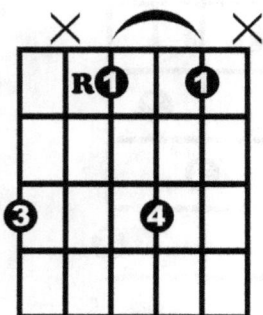

Major 6th chords contain the same notes as minor 7th chords whose roots are a minor 3rd lower. For example, a G major 6th chord contains the same notes as an E minor 7th chord.

Minor 6th (m6) Chord Shapes

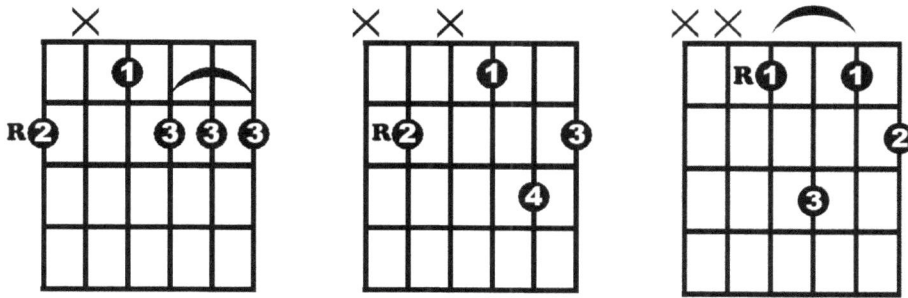

Major 6 - 9 (6/9) Chord Shapes

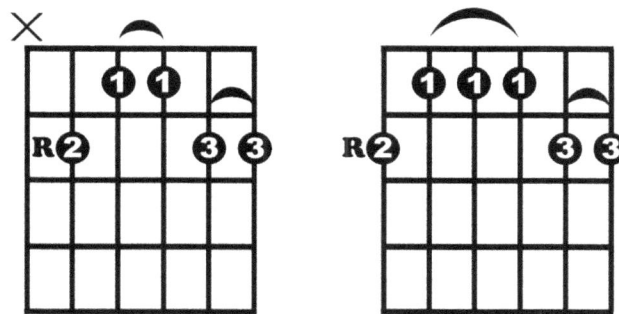

Minor 6 - 9 (m6/9) Chord Shapes

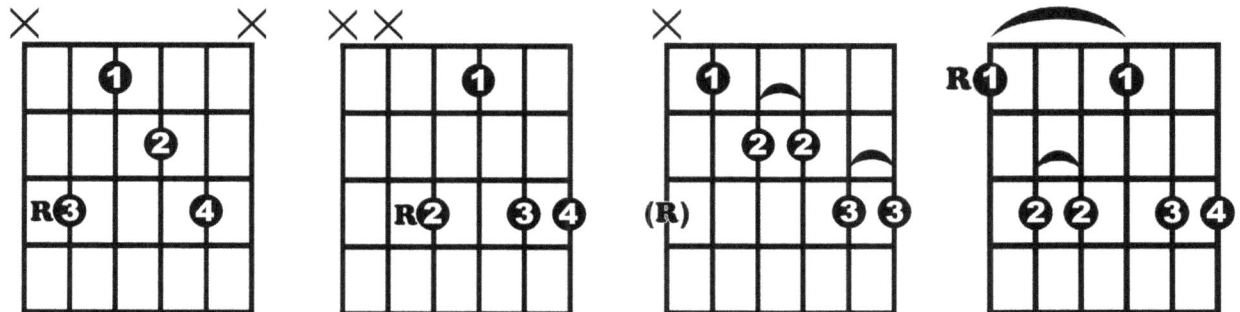

Minor / Major 7th (m(maj7)) Chord Shapes

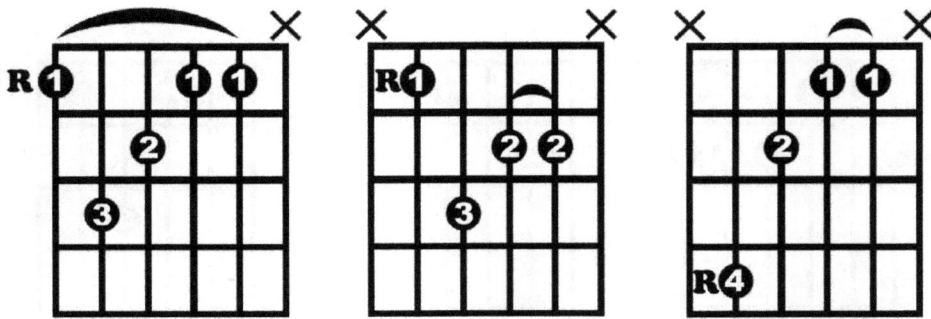

Major Add Nine (add9) Chord Shapes

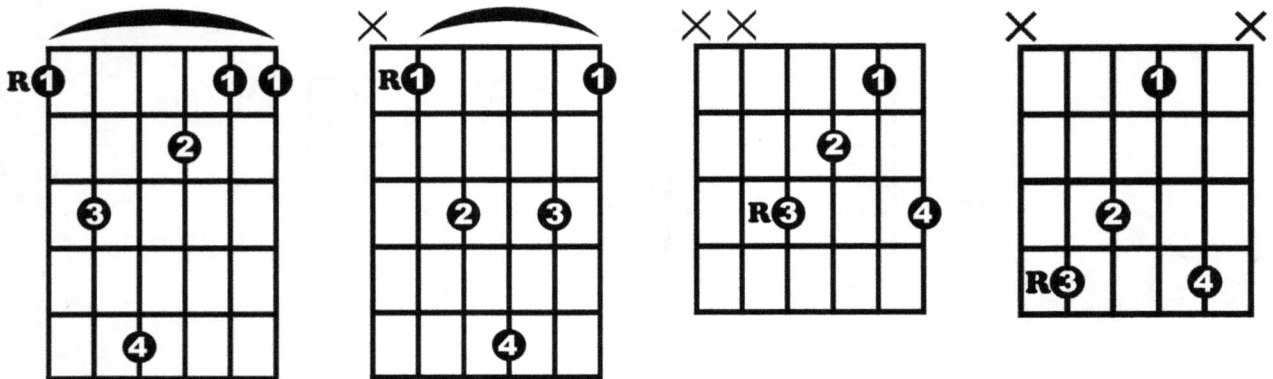

Minor Add Nine (m add9) Chord Shapes

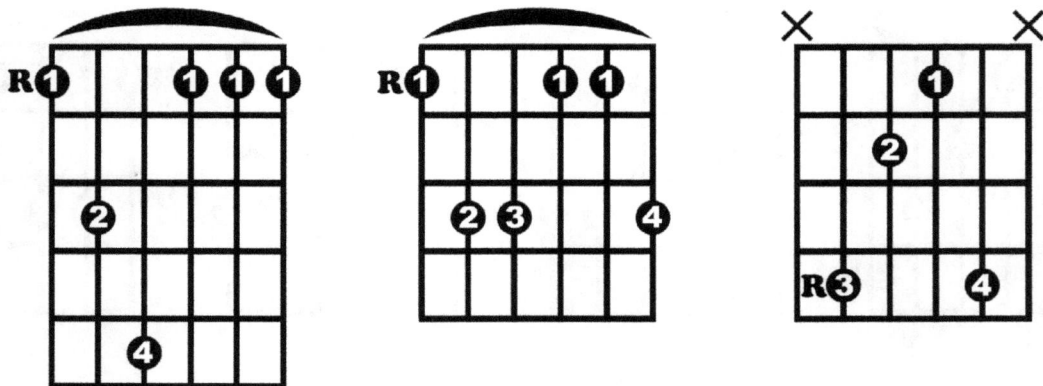

Diminished 7th (dim7 or °7) Chord Shapes

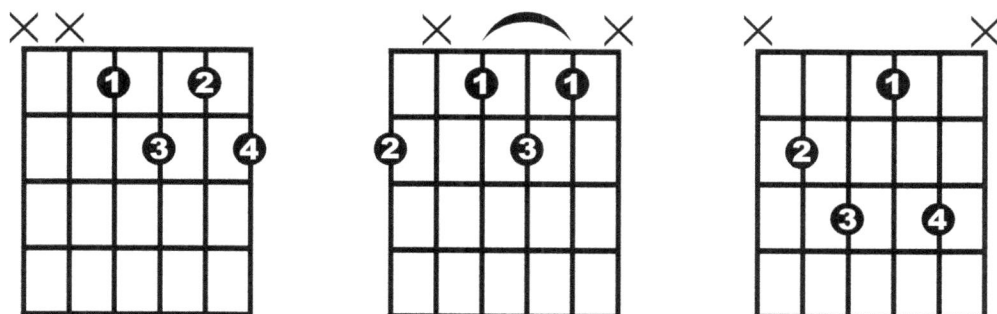

Any of the notes in a diminished seventh chord can be considered to be the root note. Another symbol for a diminished chord is a small circle: °

Dominant 9th (9) Chord Shapes

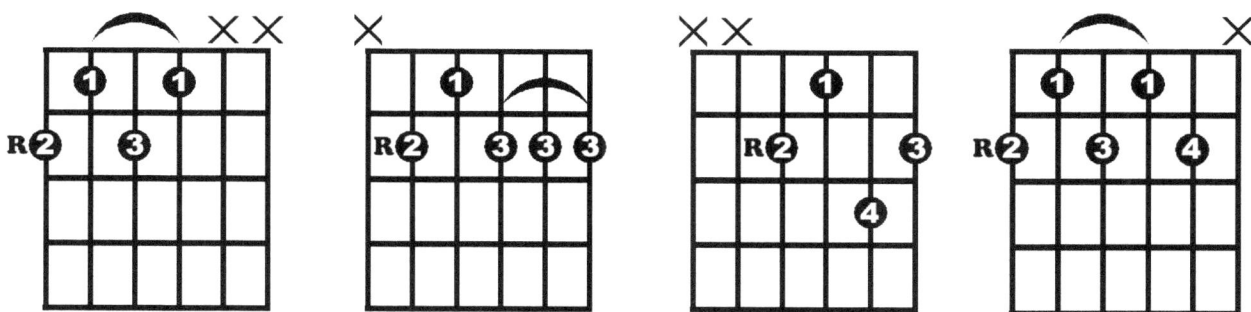

Dominant 11th (11) Chord Shapes

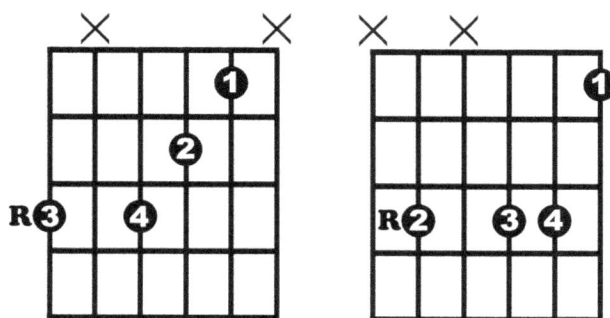

Dominant 13th (13) Chord Shapes

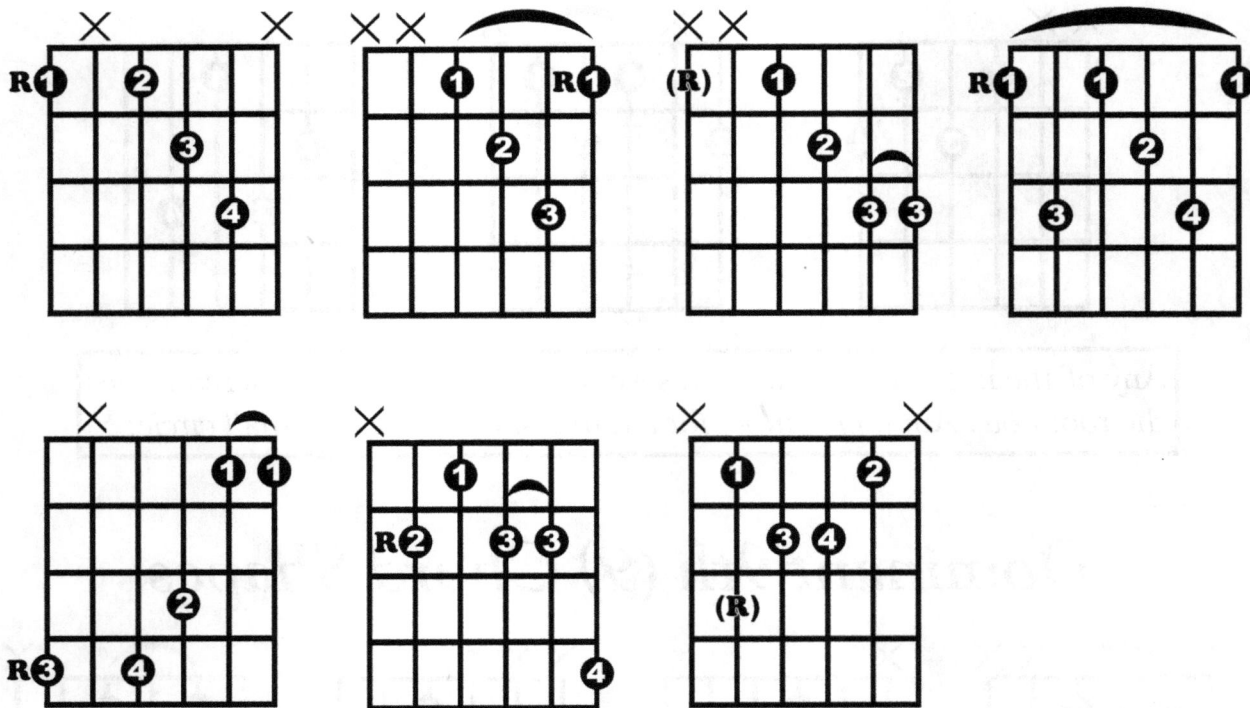

Minor 9th (m9) Chord Shapes

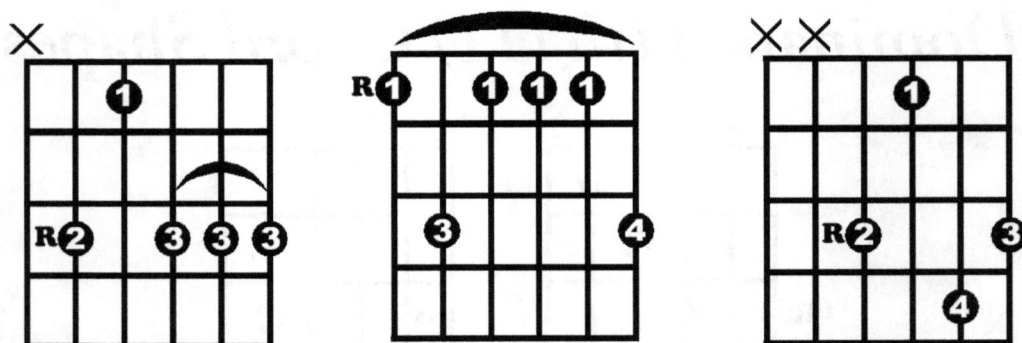

Minor 11th (m11) Chord Shapes

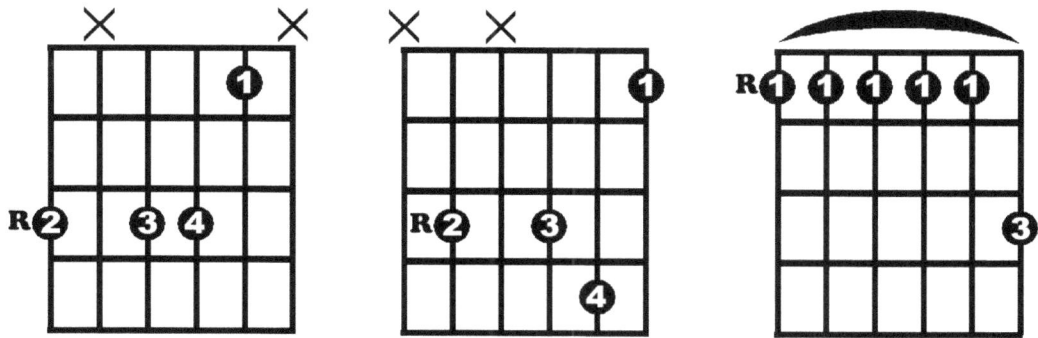

Minor 7th Flat Five (m7♭5) Chord Shapes

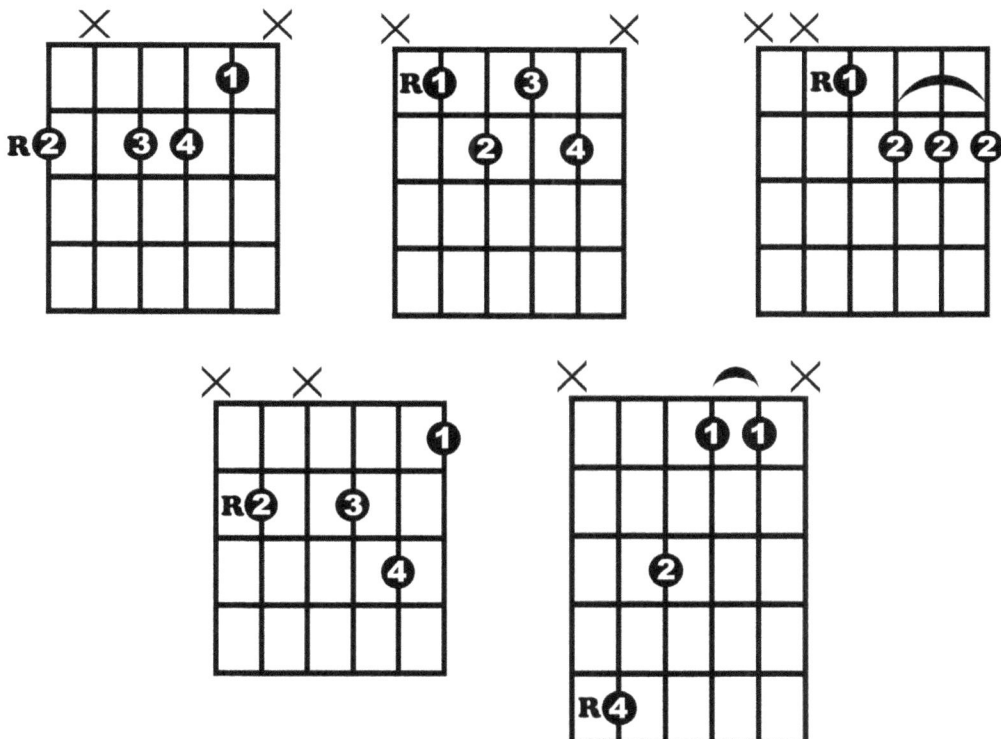

Minor 7th flat five chords are also known as 'half-diminished' chords. A commonly used symbol for a minor 7th flat five chord is a small circle with a dash through it: ∅

Three-Note Jazz Chords

Jazz guitarists can find themselves having to change chords very quickly in up-tempo numbers. To help them do this, they often play simplified versions of full chords. These three-note chords omit all but the most important notes. Some examples are provided below.

Major
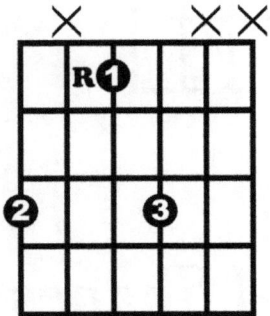

Major
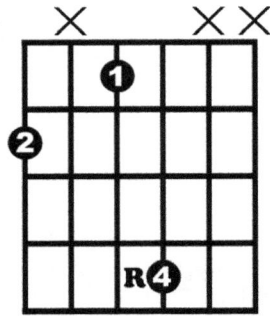

Minor
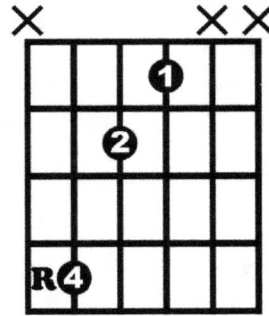

Minor
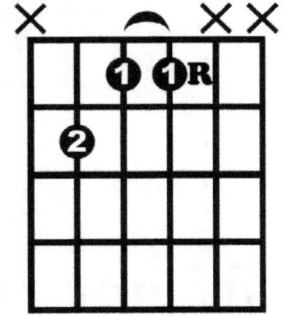

Dominant 7th
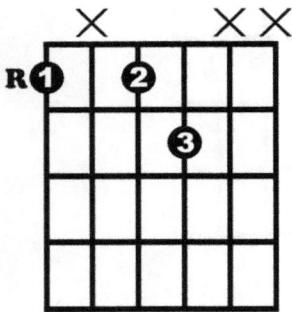

Dominant 7th
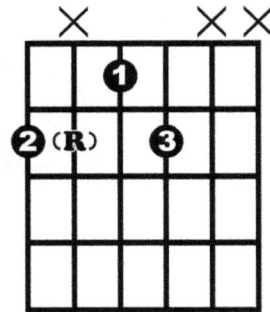

Dominant 7th
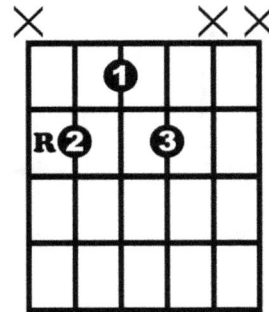

Minor 7th
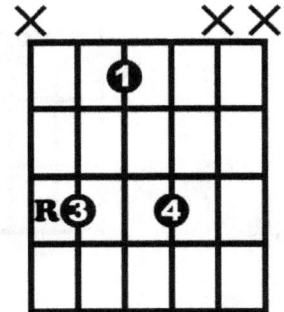

Minor 7th
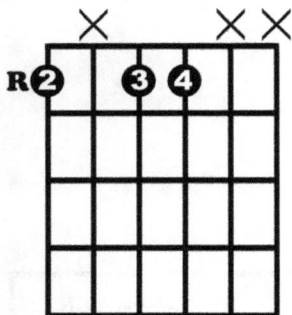

Minor 7th
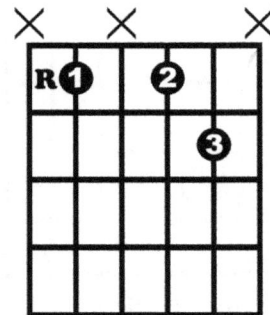

Major 7th
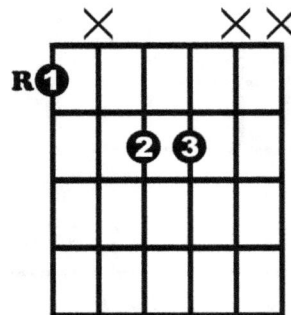

Major 7th
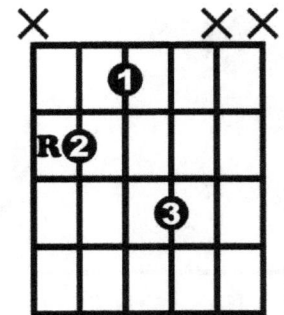

Dominant 7th Augmented (7aug or 7#5) Chord Shapes

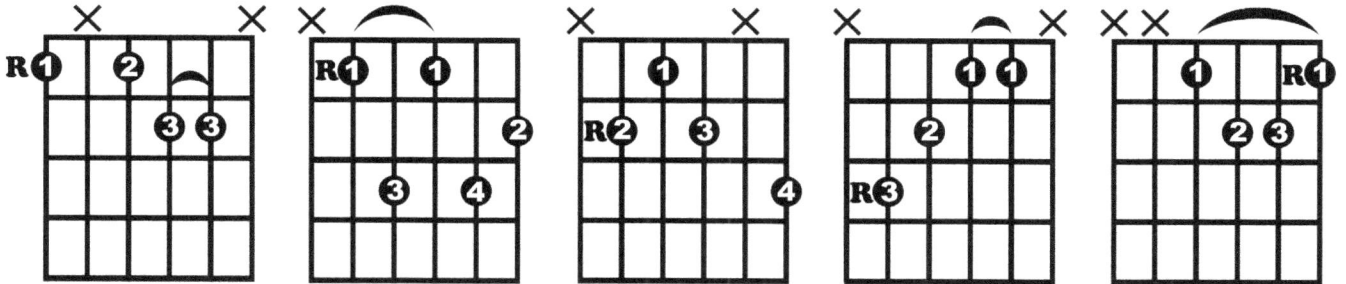

Sharp 5 chords are also called 'augmented' (aug) chords. Another symbol for an augmented chord is a plus (+) sign.

Dominant 7th Sharp Nine (7#9) Chord Shapes

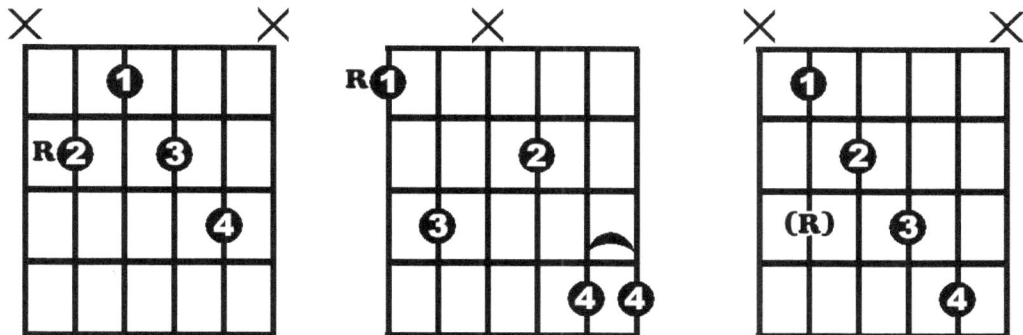

Dominant 7th Sharp Five Flat Nine (7#5♭9) Chord Shapes

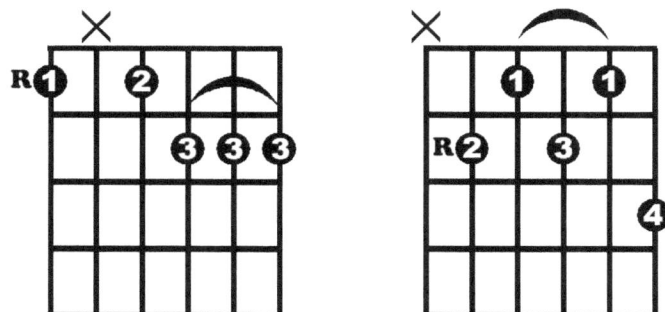

Dominant 7th Sharp Five Sharp Nine (7#5#9) Chord Shapes

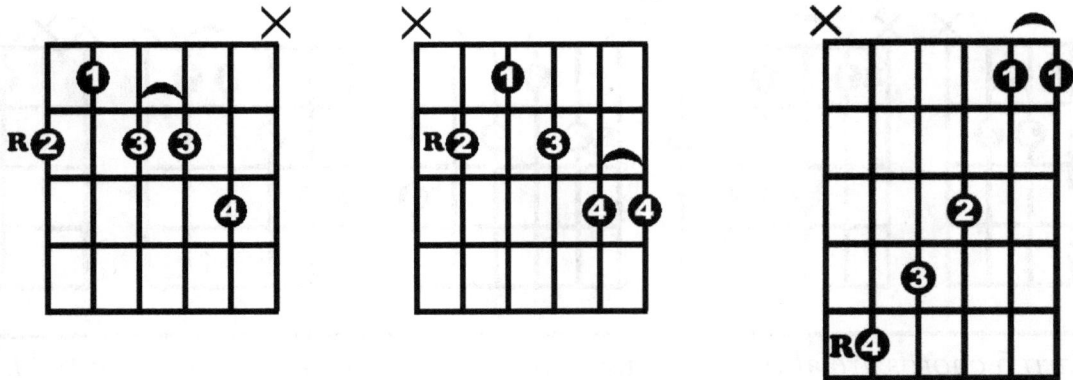

When played on their own, some of these altered chords can sound quite strange. They are mainly used in jazz, and as you play more of them, you will become accustomed to their sounds. Try playing altered dominant chords instead of standard seventh chords to get used to hearing and playing complex chords.

Dominant 7th Flat Five (7♭5) Chord Shapes

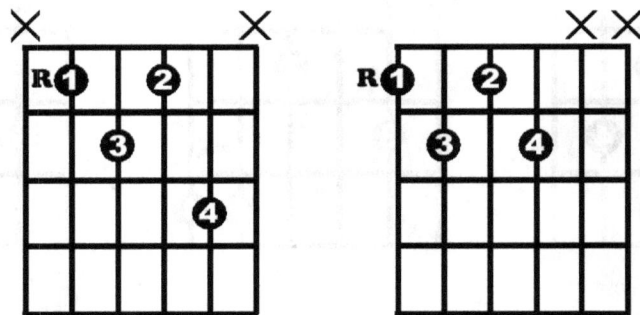

Dominant 7th Flat Nine (7♭9) Chord Shapes

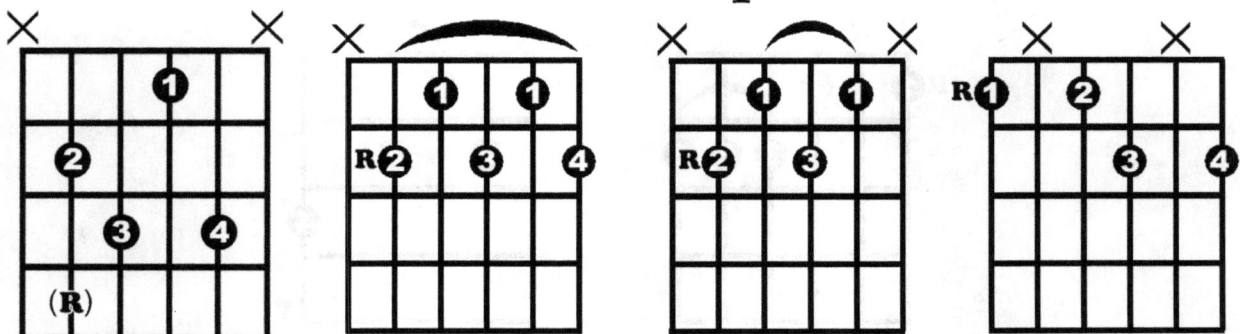

Dominant 7th Flat Five Flat Nine (7♭5♭9) Chord Shapes

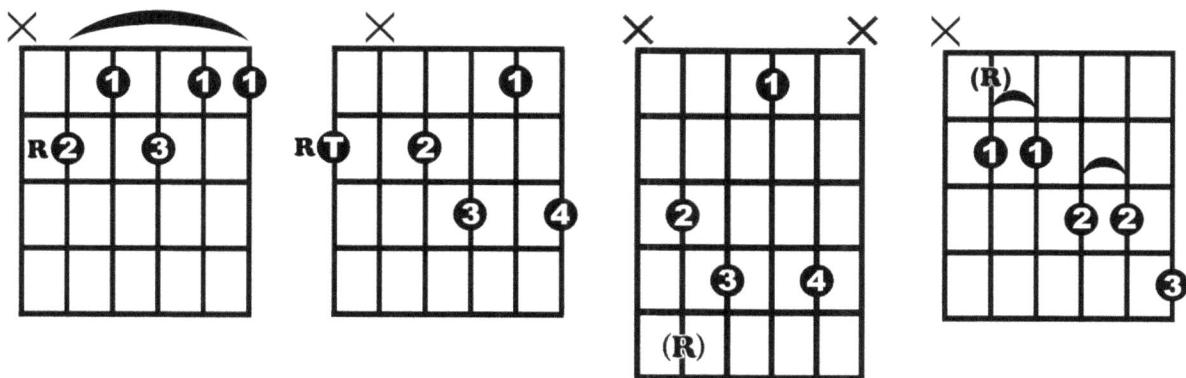

Dominant 9th Sharp Five (9♯5) Chord Shapes

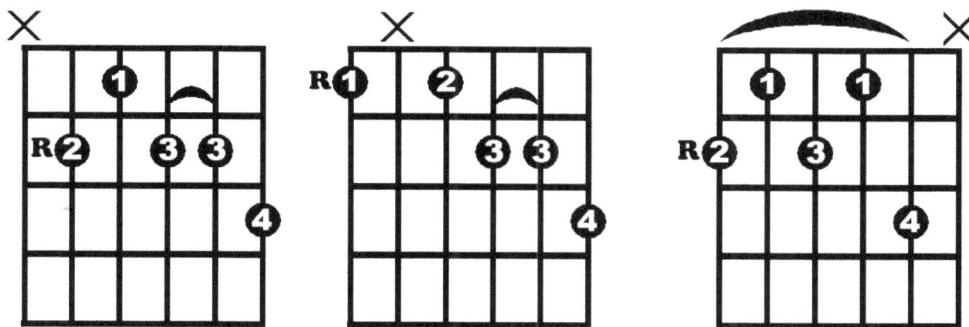

Dominant 9th Flat Five (9♭5) Chord Shapes

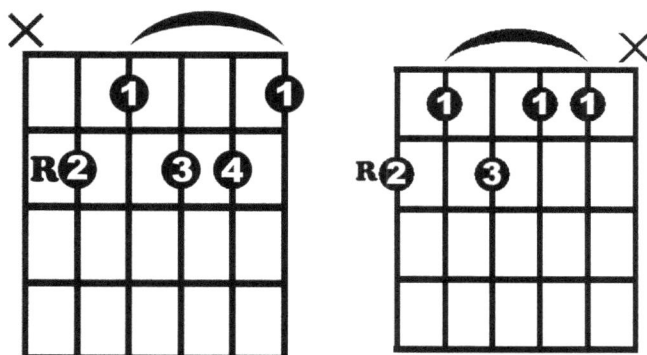

41

Dominant 13th Flat Five (13♭5)
Chord Shapes

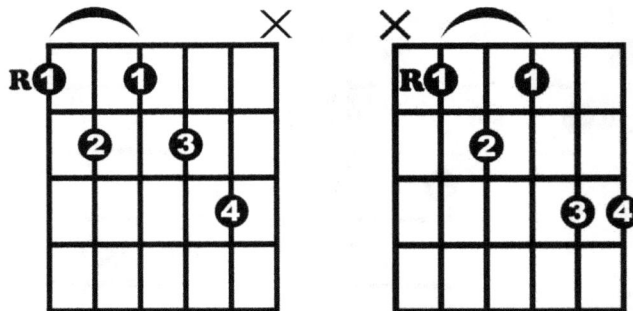

Dominant 13th Flat Nine (13♭9)
Chord Shapes

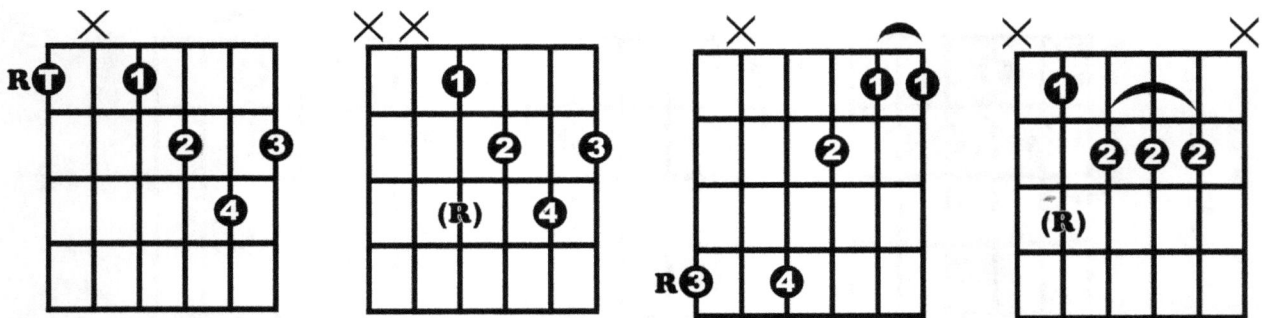

Dominant 13th Sharp Eleven (13#11)
Chord Shapes

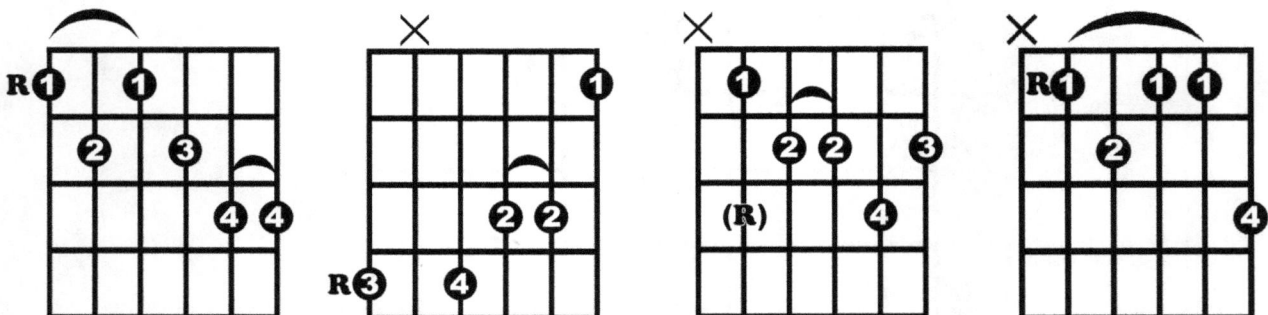

Guitar Scales

This section of the book contains guitar scales that can be used in improvisation and composition. Each scale is presented in diagram form and in notation with tab. Information on each scale is also provided.

The scale diagrams show the notes of the scale in relation to the tonic note (the tonic note is the note from which the scale is formed, i.e. the C of a C major scale).

Multiple diagrams are provided for each scale, allowing the scale to be played in different fretboard positions.

Combine two or more scale diagrams (by changing fretboard position as you play) to create multi-octave scales and longer lines.

How To Read Guitar Scale Diagrams

Like chord diagrams, scale diagrams represent the guitar fretboard. They show where the fretting fingers should be placed in order to play a scale.

The tonic notes of the scale are represented by white circles; the black circles show all of the other notes in the scale that are available at that position.

The diagram below shows how a major scale diagram is used to play a G major scale.

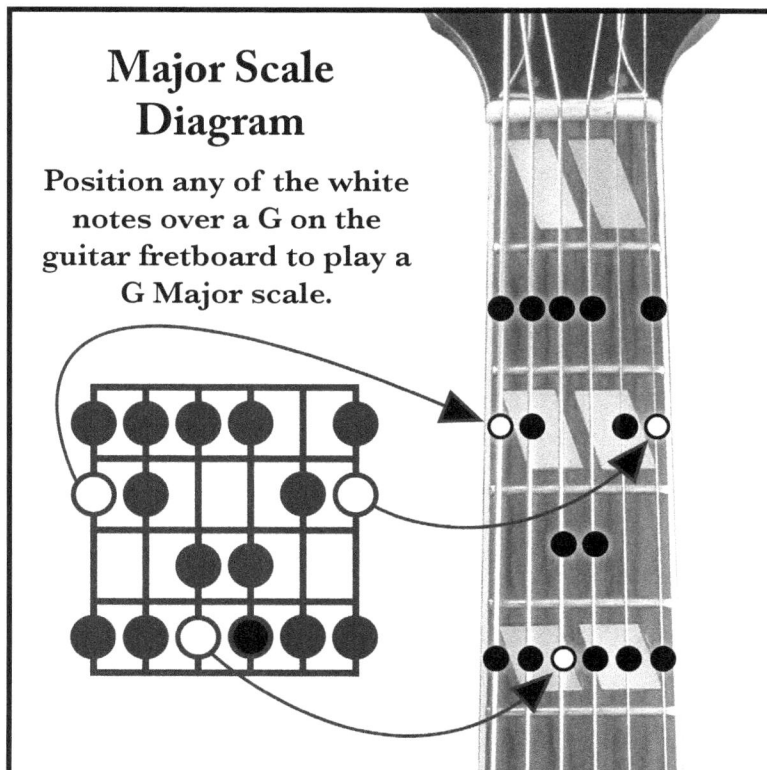

Major Scale Diagram

Position any of the white notes over a G on the guitar fretboard to play a G Major scale.

In this example the white circles (representing the root notes of the scale) are positioned over G notes on the fretboard.

The scale produced by playing up from one white note to another is a G major scale.

If you were to position your hand so that the white circles were over A notes on the fretboard, the same shape would produce an A major scale.

If necessary, use the guitar fretboard diagram on page 9 to position the white notes over the tonic note you need.

When playing just the scale, start and end on white notes. Play up to the top note then play back down the scale to the starting note. The top note is usually only played once.

When using the scale in improvisation, all of the notes (black and white) can be used. (While improvising, you would not necessarily play the notes in the scale sequentially, therefore the diagrams show **all** of the notes in the scale available in that position on the fretboard.)

Some scale diagrams can be used for more than one tonic note (e.g. diminished scale diagrams). Where this occurs, all of the potential tonic / root notes are shown as white circles.

Scale Spellings

Scale spellings show the notes of a scale compared to those of a major scale. They are useful for learning and comparing scales.

Examples of scale spellings are shown in the chart below:

Scale Type	Scale Spelling	Notes With Tonic Of C
Major	1, 2, 3, 4, 5, 6, 7	C, D, E, F, G, A, B
Dorian	1, 2, ♭3, 4, 5, 6, ♭7	C, D, E♭, F, G, A, B♭
Phrygian	1, 2, 3, ♯4, 5, 6, 7	C, D, E, F♯, G, A, B

Major Scale / Ionian Modal Scale

The 'standard', familiar sounding scale, upon which the scale spelling system is based. Many famous melodies have been written using the major scale, and it is also commonly used in improvisation. Major scales can also be referred to as Ionian modal scales.

Scale spelling: 1, 2, 3, 4, 5, 6, 7

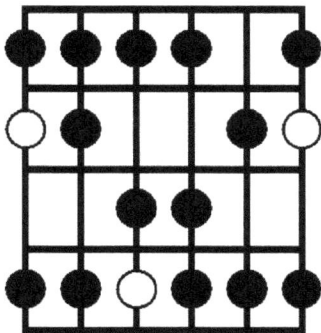

1.

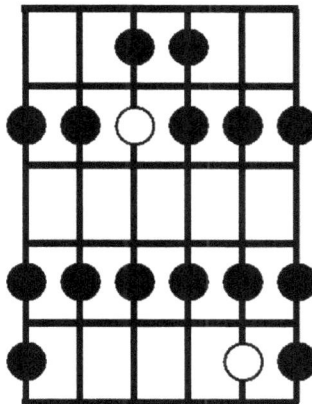

2.

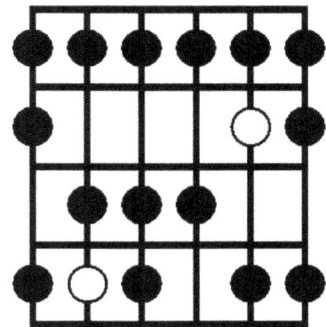

3.

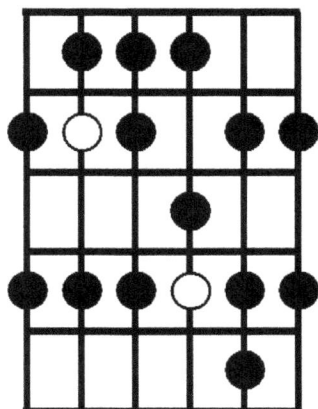

4.

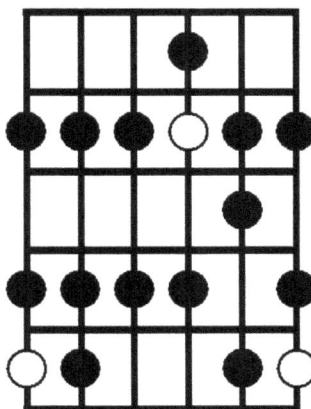

5.

Pentatonic Minor Scale

The pentatonic minor scale forms the basis of many famous guitar solos and riffs. It is used by practically every lead guitarist in every musical style, and should be among the first guitar scales a beginner guitarist learns.

Scale spelling: 1, ♭3, 4, 5, ♭7

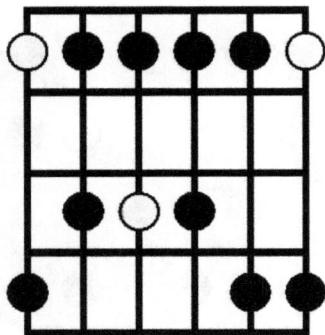

1.

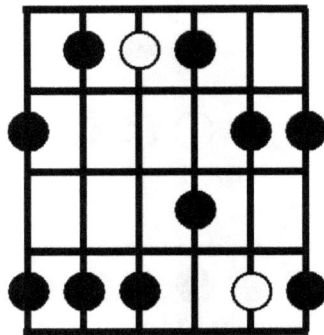

2.

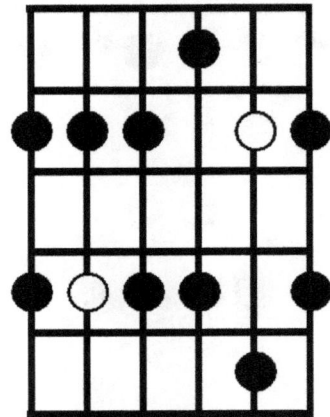

3.

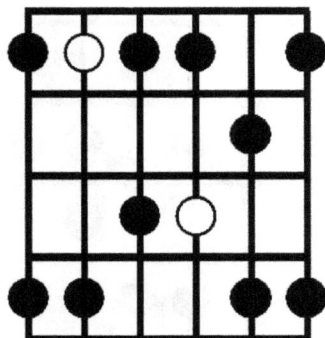

4.

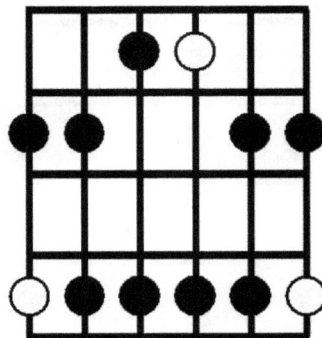

5.

Pentatonic Major Scale

A widely used guitar scale which produces a clear, melodic sound. Ideal for soloing over major chord sequences. Often used in country and rock music. Notice that the shapes are the same as those of the pentatonic minor, but that the root notes are in different positions.

Scale Spelling: 1, 2, 3, 5, 6

Blues Scale

One of the most frequently used lead guitar scales, and not just in blues music. The blues scale is the same scale as a pentatonic minor, but with an additional note – the flattened fifth. This is known as the 'blues' note, and produces the characteristic blues sound.

Scale spelling: 1, ♭3, 4, ♭5, 5, ♭7

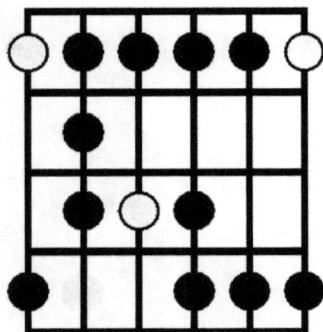

1.

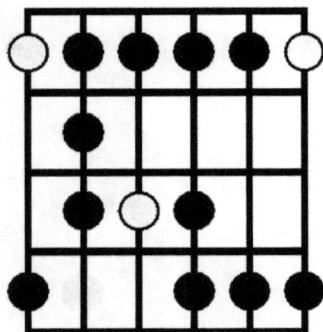

2.

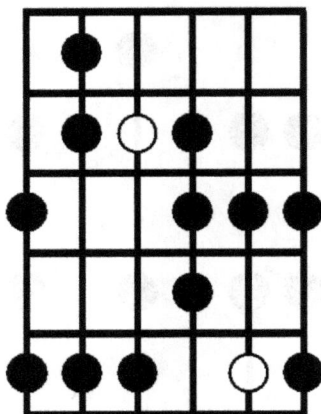

3.

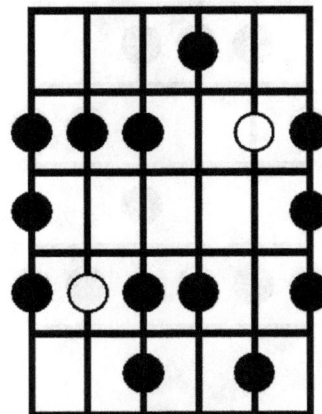

4.

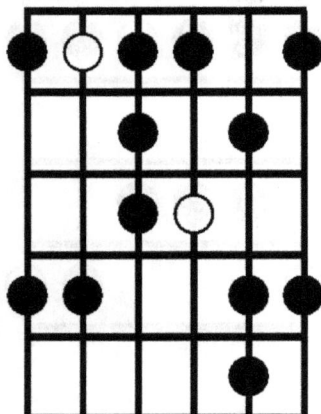

5.

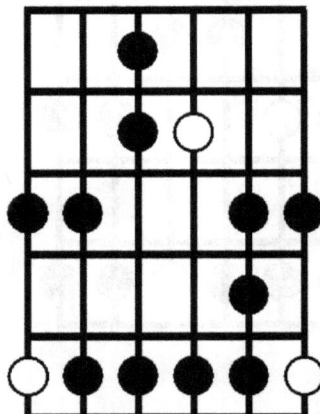

Dorian Modal Scale

The Dorian mode is the second mode of a major scale. It has a distinctive minor tonality and is often used when improvising over minor seventh chords.

Scale spelling: 1, 2, ♭3, 4, 5, 6, ♭7

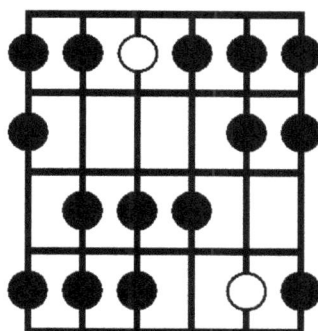

1.
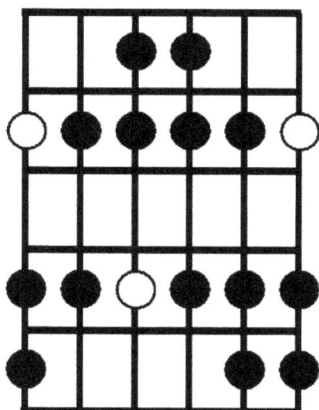

2.

3.
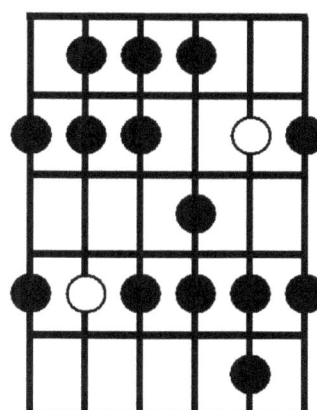

4.
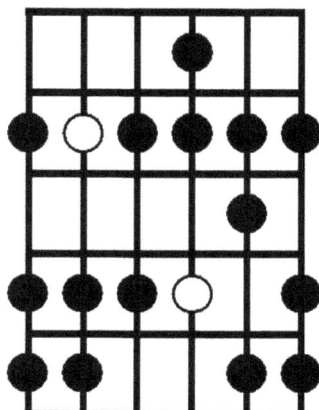

5.
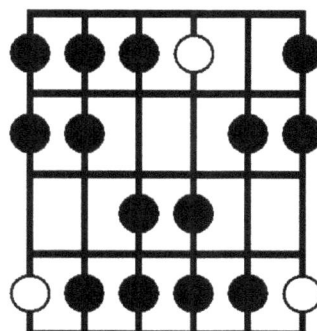

Phrygian Modal Scale

The Phrygian mode is the third mode of a major scale. It is a minor scale, with a slightly 'Eastern' or Spanish sound. It is often used by rock guitarists for soloing over power chords.

Scale spelling: 1, ♭2, ♭3, 4, 5, ♭6, ♭7

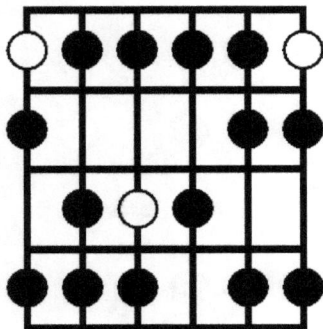

1.

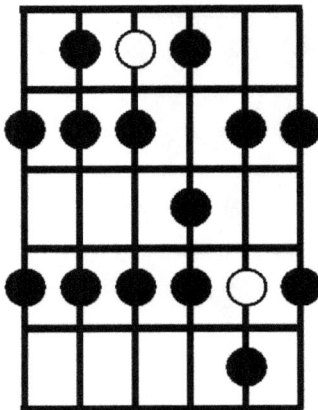

2.

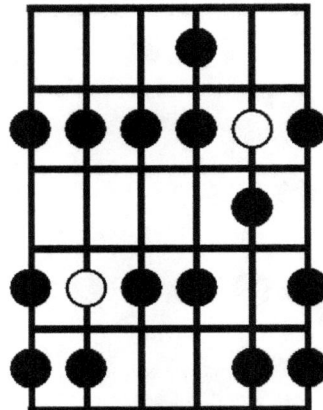

3.

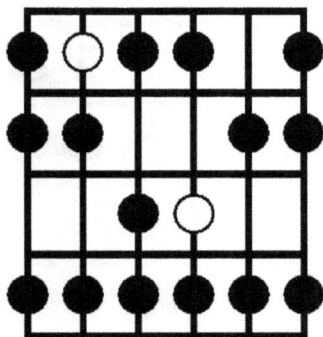

4.

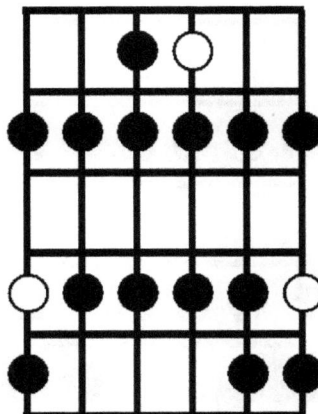

5.

Lydian Modal Scale

The Lydian mode is the fourth mode of a major scale. It is the same as a normal major scale but with a raised fourth note; this forms a tritone (augmented fourth interval) with the tonic note, giving the scale its unique sound.

Scale spelling: 1, 2, 3, ♯4, 5, 6, 7

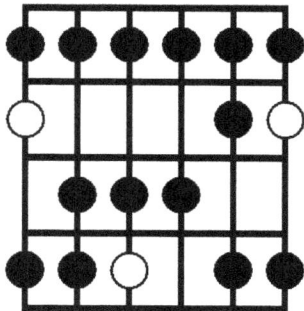

1.

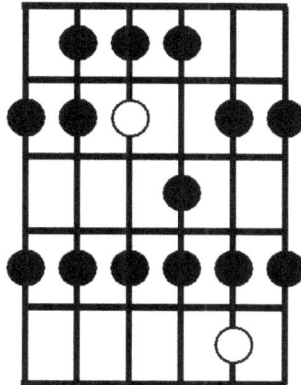

2.

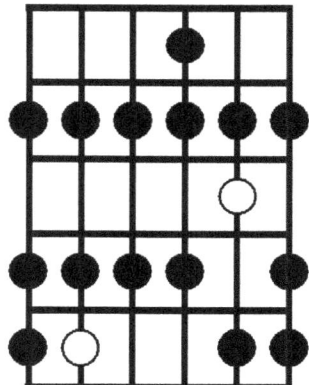

3.

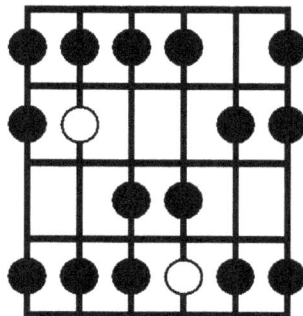

4.

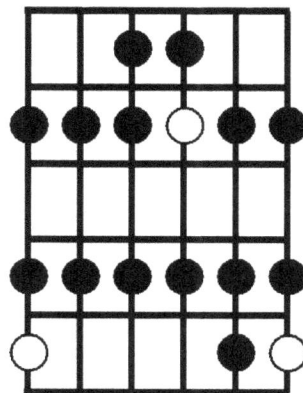

5.

Mixolydian Modal Scale

The Mixolydian mode is the fifth mode of a major scale. Its minor (flattened) seventh note makes it suitable for playing over dominant seventh chords whose root is the same as the tonic note of the scale.

Scale spelling: 1, 2, 3, 4, 5, 6, ♭7

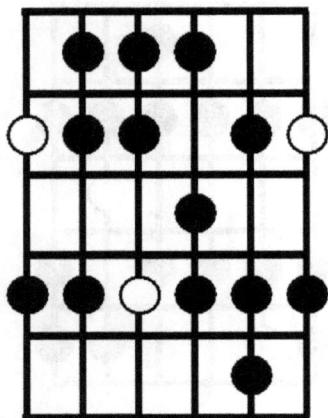

1.

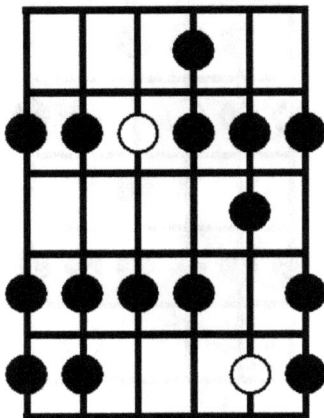

2.

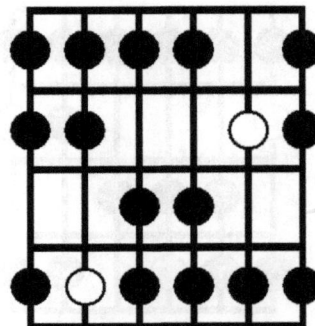

3.

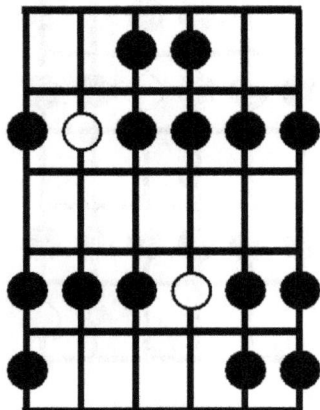

4.

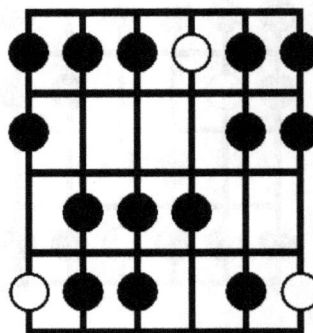

5.

Aeolian Modal Scale / Natural Minor Scale

The Aeolian mode is the sixth mode of a major scale. It is also known as the natural minor scale and can be used to solo over minor chord sequences.

Scale spelling: 1, 2, ♭3, 4, 5, ♭6, ♭7

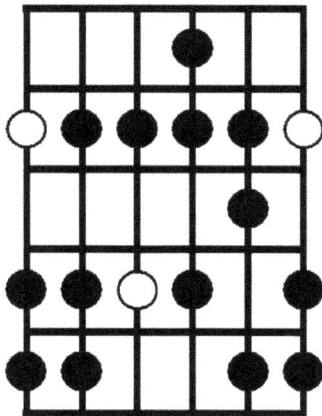

1.

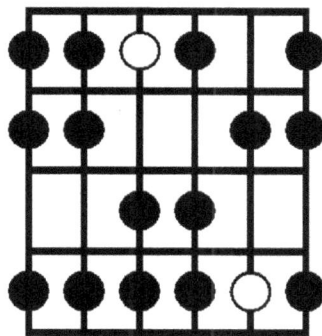

2.

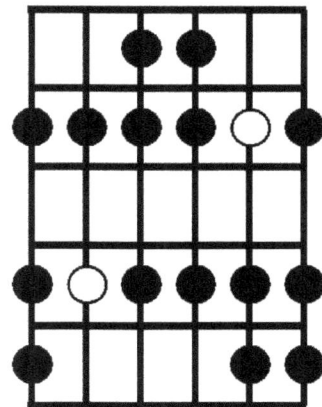

3.

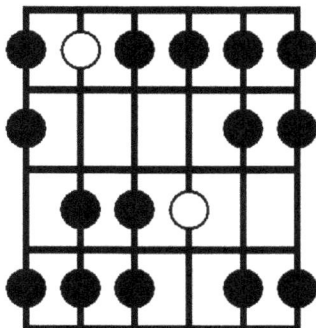

4.

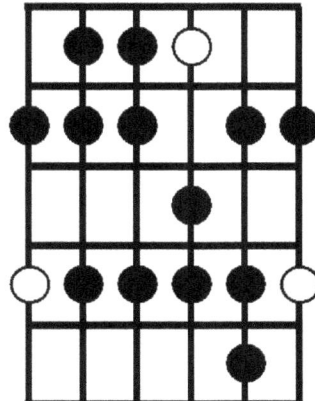

5.

Locrian Modal Scale

The Locrian mode is the seventh mode of a major scale. It can be used to improvise over minor seven flat five chords.

Scale spelling: 1, ♭2, ♭3, 4, ♭5, ♭6, ♭7

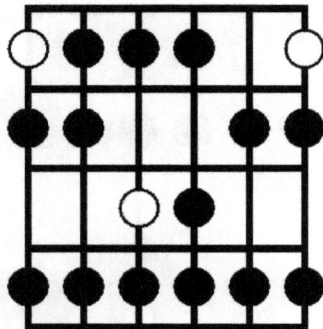

1.

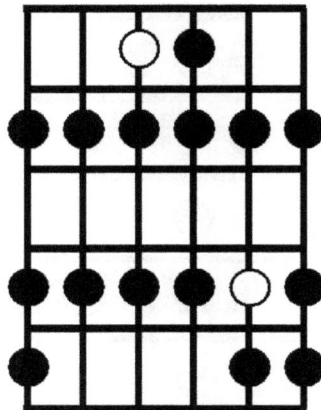

2.

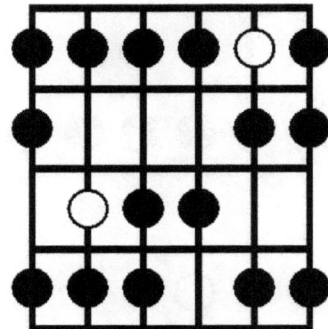

3.

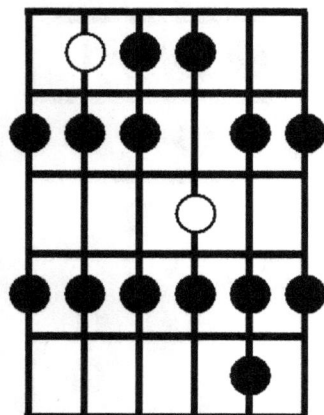

4.

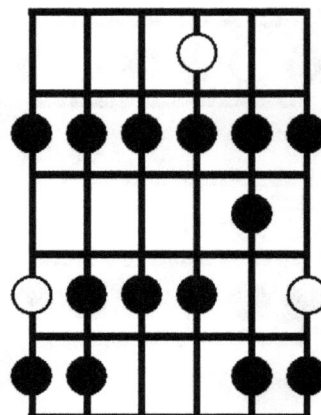

5.

Harmonic Minor Scale

The harmonic minor scale has a more 'classical' sound than other minor scales, and can be used to add interest to lead lines.

Scale spelling: 1, 2, ♭3, 4, 5, ♭6, 7

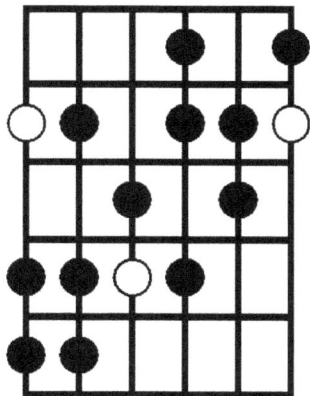

1.

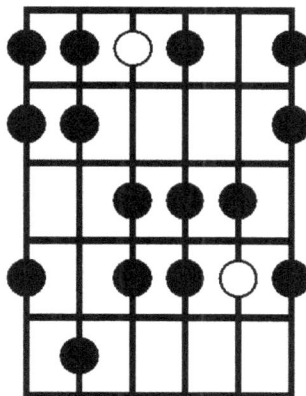

2.

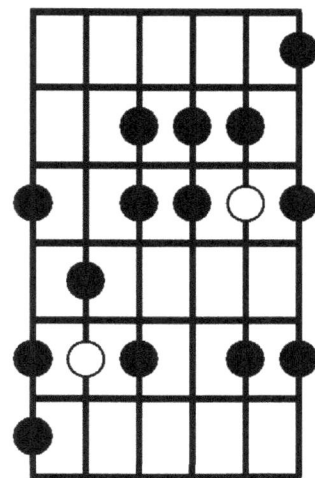

3.

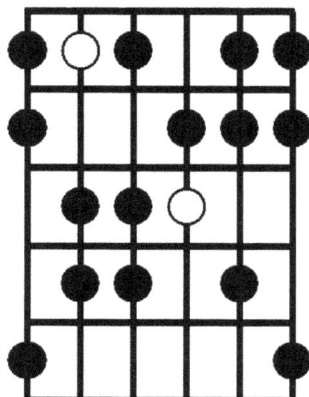

4.

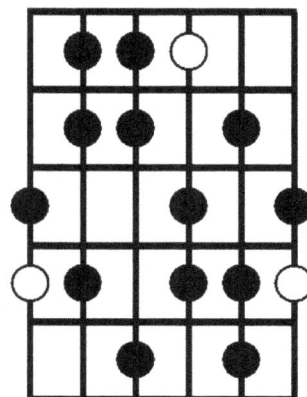

5.

Jazz Minor Scale / Melodic Minor Scale

The jazz minor scale is also known as the melodic minor scale, although strictly speaking it is only the same as the descending form of the melodic minor used in traditional 'classical' music theory. The jazz minor is a good scale to use when improvising over minor sixth chords. If the seventh note of a jazz minor scale is used as the tonic note, it becomes an altered scale. Compare the two scales to see the relationship.

Scale spelling: 1, 2, ♭3, 4, 5, 6, 7

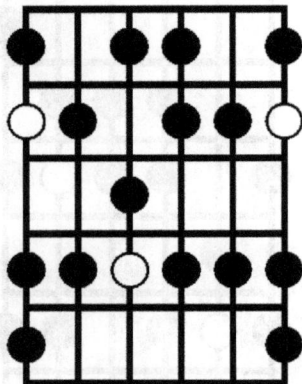

1.

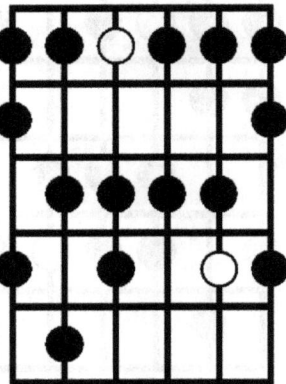

2.

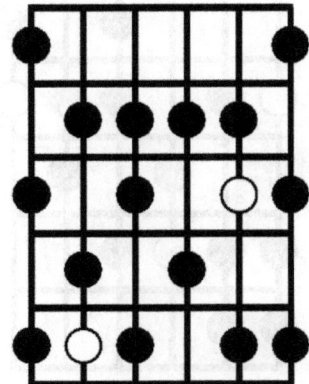

3.

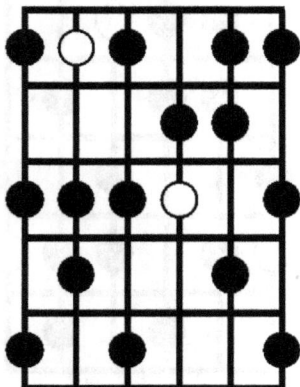

4.

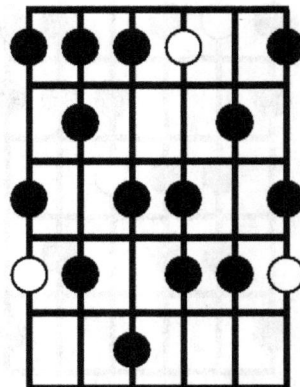

5.

Phrygian Dominant Scale

The Phrygian dominant scale is also known as the 'Spanish Gypsy' or 'Freygish' scale (note that the double harmonic scale is sometimes called the Spanish gypsy scale too). The Phrygian dominant scale can also be thought of as being the fifth mode of a harmonic minor scale – the scale shapes are the same but the tonic notes are different depending on which scale is being played. The Phrygian dominant scale produces an Eastern sound that can add interest to your improvisation.

Scale spelling: 1, ♭2, 3, 4, 5, ♭6, ♭7

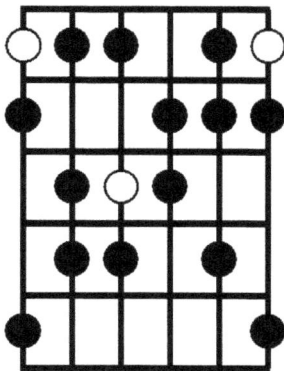

1.

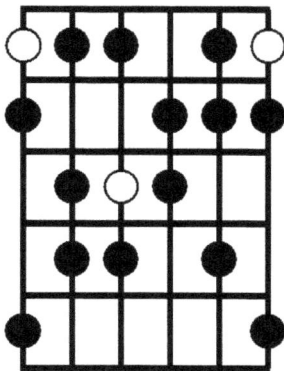

2.

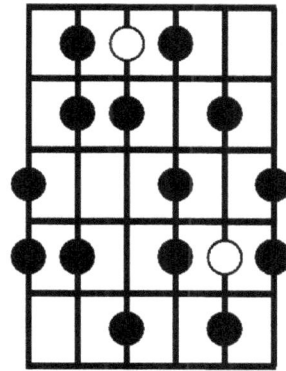

3.

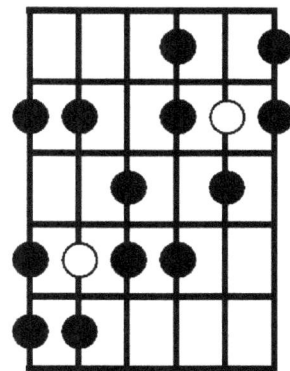

4.

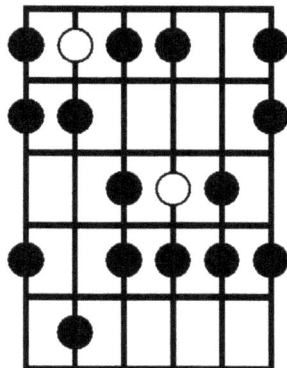

5.

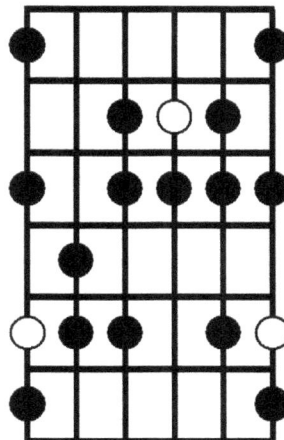

Double Harmonic Scale

The double harmonic scale is another Eastern-sounding scale. It goes by several other names, including the Arabic Scale, (Spanish) Gypsy Scale and Byzantine Scale.

Scale spelling: 1, ♭2, 3, 4, 5, ♭6, 7

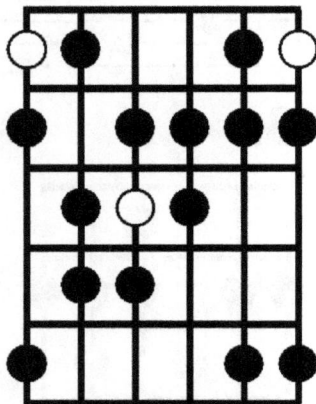

1.

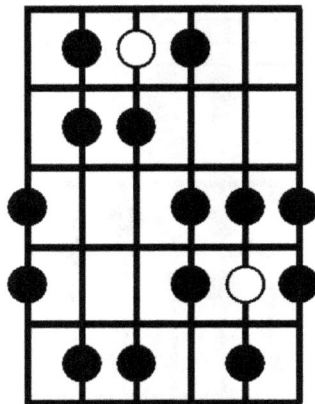

2.

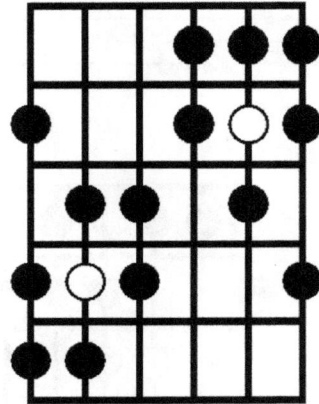

3.

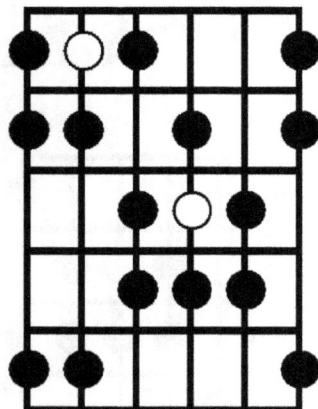

4.

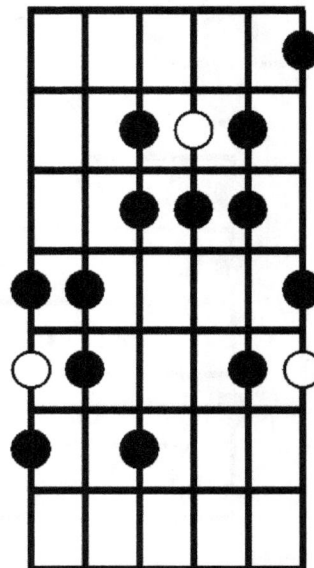

5.

Persian Scale

The Persian scale can add an exotic color to your improvisations. It is very similar to the double harmonic and Phrygian dominant scales.

Persian Scale Spelling: 1, ♭2, 3, 4, ♭5, ♭6, 7

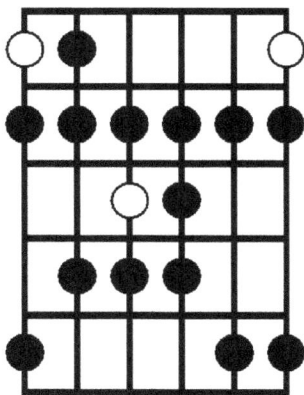

1.

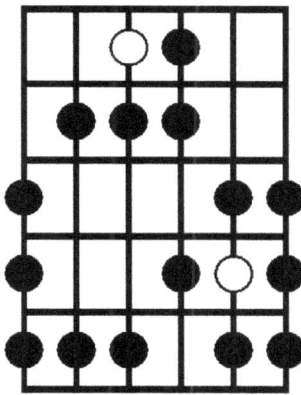

2.

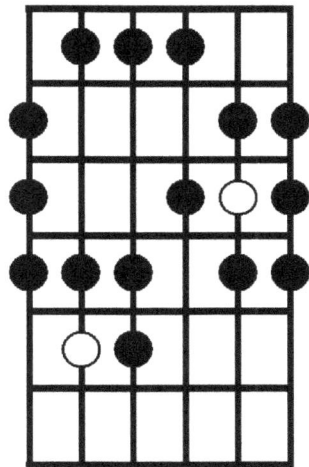

3.

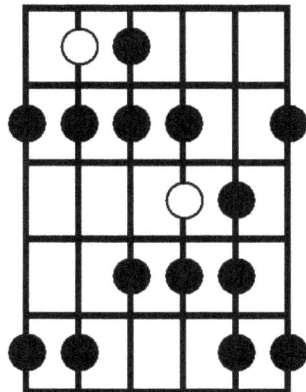

4.

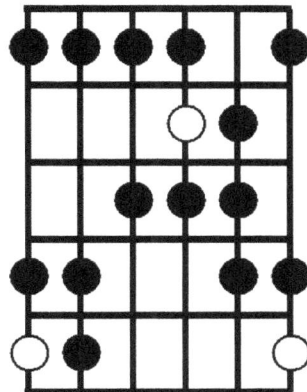

5.

Neapolitan Minor Scale

The Neapolitan minor scale is another exotic scale that could be used to spice up a solo, or perhaps to provide inspiration for composition.

Scale spelling: 1, ♭2, ♭3, 4, 5, ♭6, 7

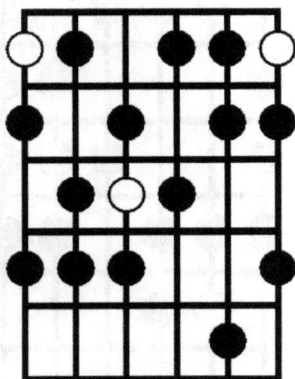

1.

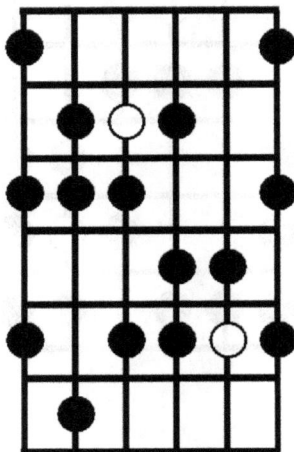

2.

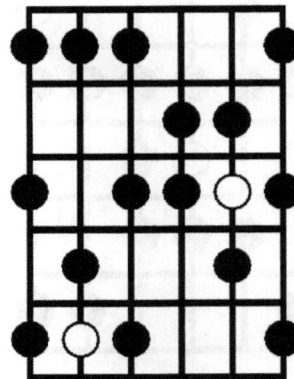

3.

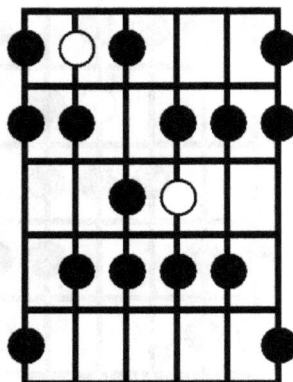

4.

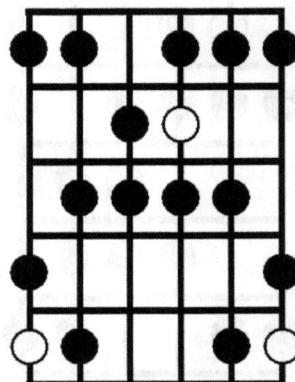

5.

Neapolitan Major Scale

The Neapolitan Major scale, despite its name, actually has a minor tonality. It differs from the Neapolitan minor scale only by having a non-flattened sixth note.

Scale spelling: 1, ♭2, ♭3, 4, 5, 6, 7

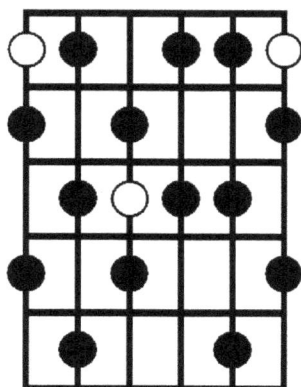

1.

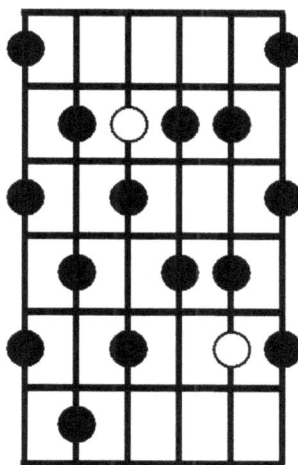

2.

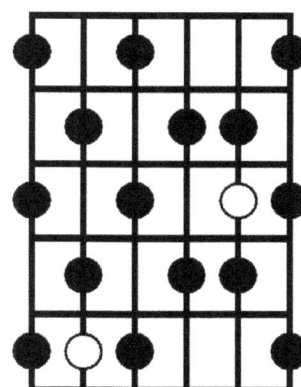

3.

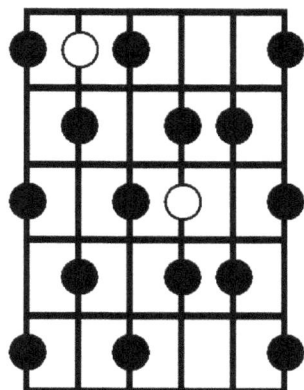

4.

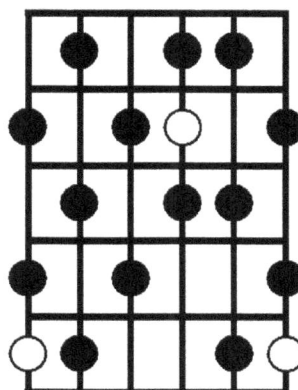

5.

Bebop Dominant Scale

The bebop dominant scale is similar to a Mixolydian modal scale, but has an additional note: the major seventh. Bebop scales have an extra note to enable jazz musicians to create smooth lines in which chord tones always fall on the beat.

Scale spelling: 1, 2, 3, 4, 5, 6, ♭7, 7

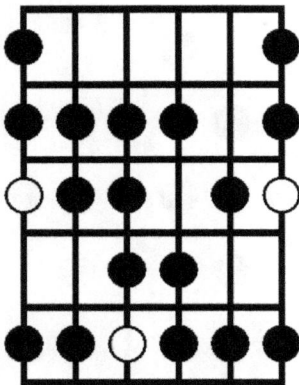

1.

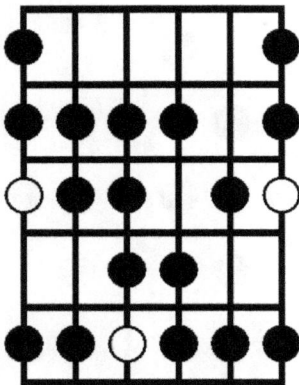

2.

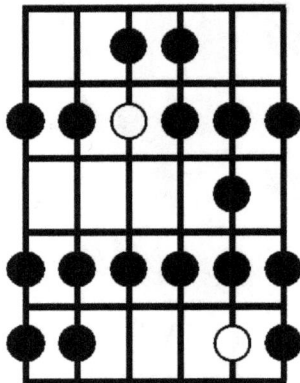

3.

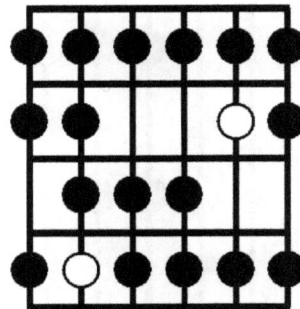

4.

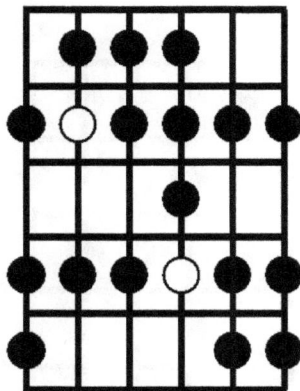

5.

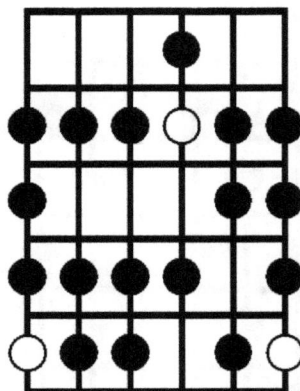

Bebop Minor Scale

The bebop minor scale is related to the Dorian modal scale, but like the bebop dominant scale has an extra note to allow flowing jazz lines. The scale shapes are the same as those for the bebop dominant (both scales use the same notes if a bebop minor scale is played over a II chord and a bebop dominant over a V7 chord).

Scale spelling: 1, 2, ♭3, 3, 4, 5, 6, ♭7

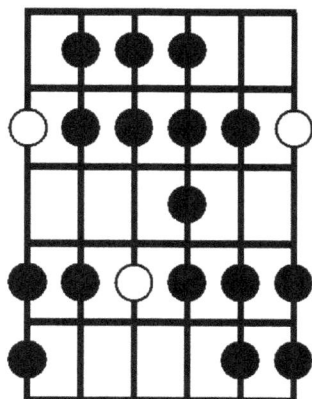

1.

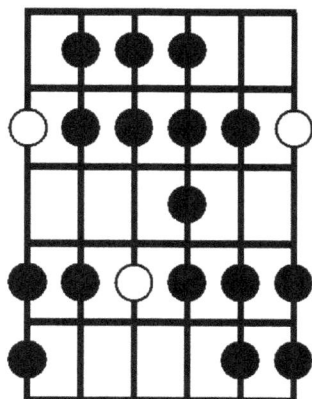

2.

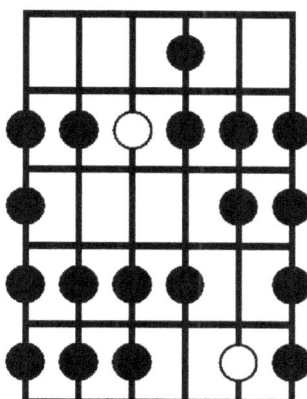

3.

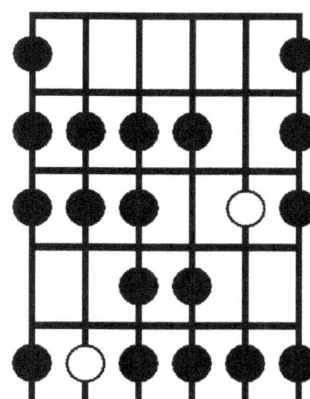

4.

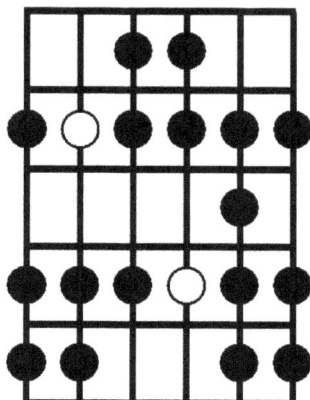

5.

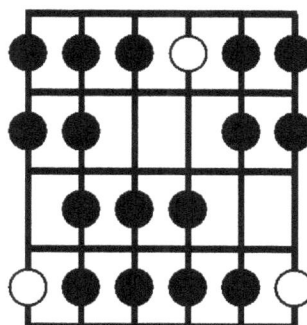

Bebop Major Scale

The bebop major scale is the same as a standard major scale, but with an extra note: the augmented fifth. As with the other bebop scales, the additional note allows jazz improvisors to create fluid lines. Try playing the scale with a swing feel over a major chord with the same root to get a feel for the jazz sound.

Scale spelling: 1, 2, 3, 4, 5, #5, 6, 7

1.

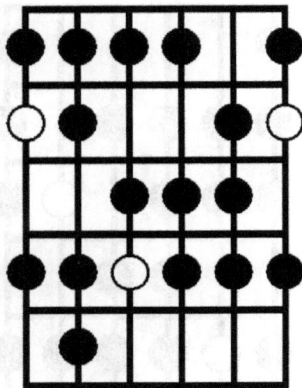

2.

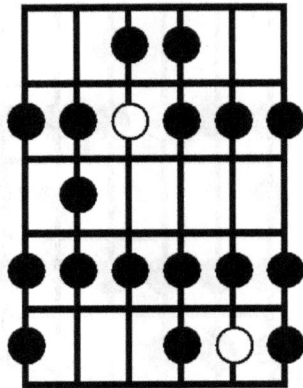

3.

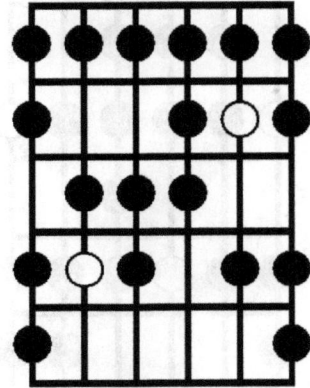

4.

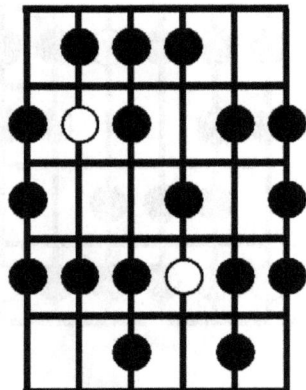

5.

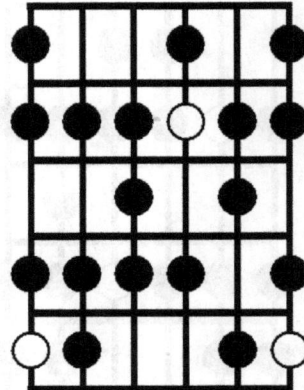

Altered Scale

The altered scale is the same as a jazz minor scale that starts from the seventh degree. It is mainly used to improvise over dominant chords*. The altered scale is so-called because it contains every possible altered note (sharpened and flattened 5ths, 9ths and 11ths). These altered notes are used by improvisors to create jazzy-sounding tensions in their lines.

Scale spelling: 1, ♭2, ♭3, ♭4, ♭5, ♭6, ♭7

1.

2.

3.

4.

5.

* Most guitarists simply play a jazz minor scale a semitone higher than the dominant chord – it can then be considered to be an altered scale and only one scale needs to be learned.

Lydian Augmented Scale

The Lydian augmented scale is a variation of the Lydian modal scale. It has an augmented fifth and can be used over major chords with raised fifths. It can also be used to solo over dominant seventh flat-five chords by using the Lydian augmented scale whose tonic is the seventh of the chord, or over altered dominant chords by using the scale whose tonic is the third of the chord (in this case it is the same as an altered scale).

Scale spelling: 1, 2, 3, #4, #5, 6, 7

1.

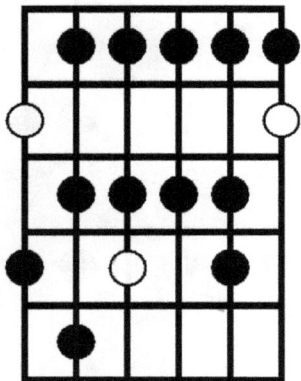

2.

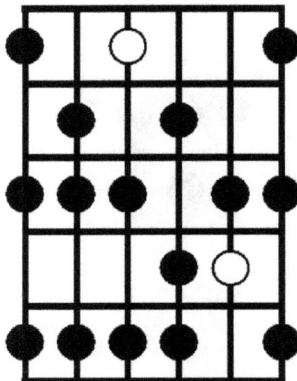

3.

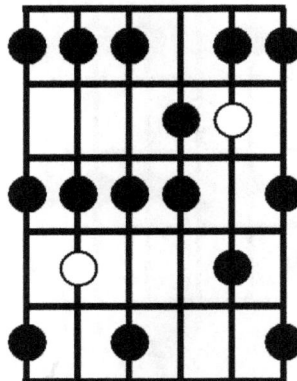

4.

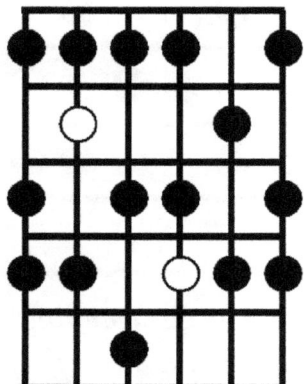

5.

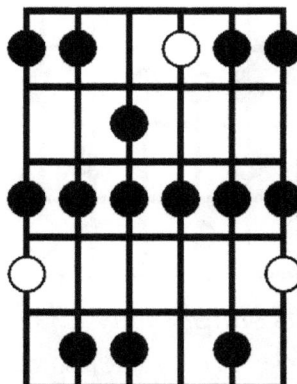

Mixolydian #4 / Lydian ♭7 Scale

A jazzy scale that has two names; it can either be thought of as a Mixolydian scale with a sharpened fourth, or as a Lydian scale with a flattened seventh note. This scale can be used over dominant chords with the same root as the tonic of the scale, and works particularly well over seven flat-five or seven sharp-eleven chords.

Scale spelling: 1, 2, 3, #4, 5, 6, ♭7

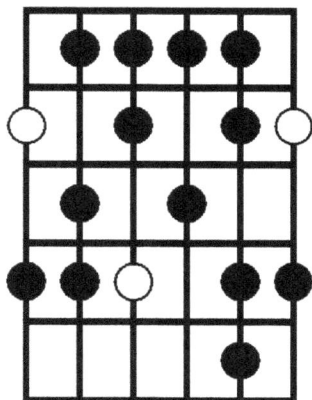

1.

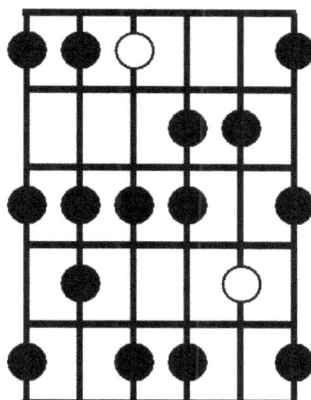

2.

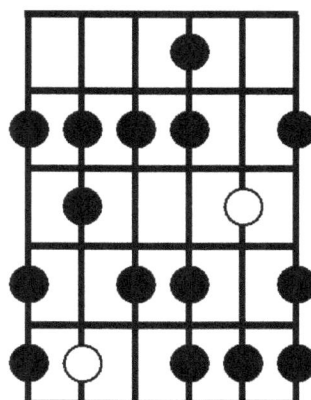

3.

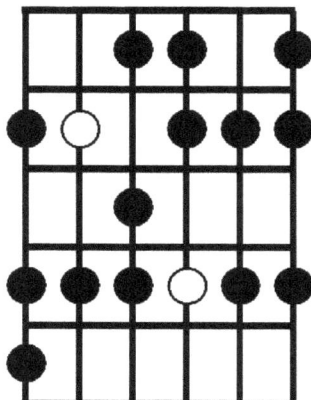

4.

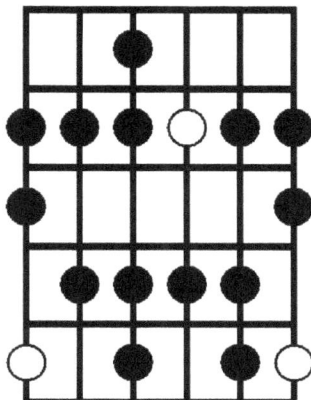

5.

Locrian #2 Scale

This scale is a variation of the Locrian modal scale, and like that scale, can be used to improvise over minor seven flat-five chords whose root is the same as the tonic of the scale.

Scale spelling: 1, 2, ♭3, 4, ♭5, ♭6, ♭7

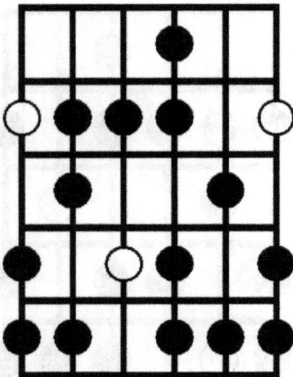
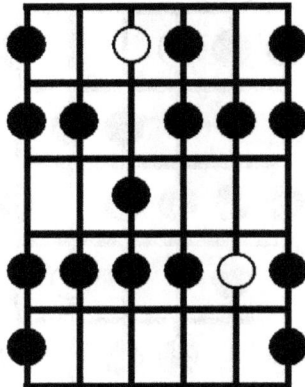
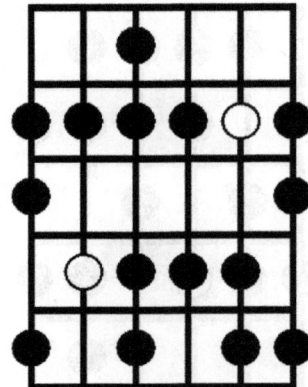

1.   **2.**   **3.**

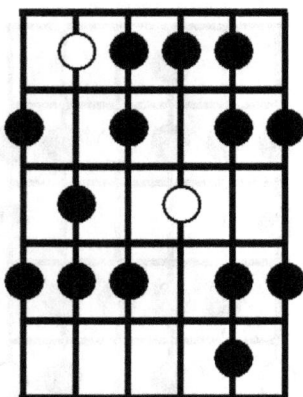
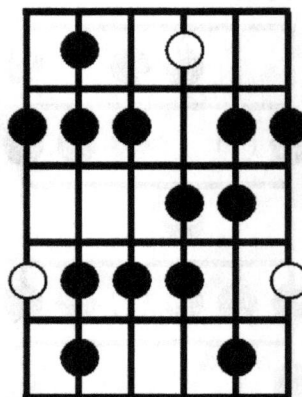

4.   **5.**

Diminished Scale

Diminished scales move in alternate whole and half-steps. They can be used to improvise over diminished chords with the same root as the tonic of the scale. They are also used over dominant chords: use the diminished scale a half-step higher than the root of the chord. Used in the second way, diminished scales create tensions that can give the line a jazz sound.

Scale spelling: 1, 2, ♭3, 4, ♭5, ♭6, 6, 7

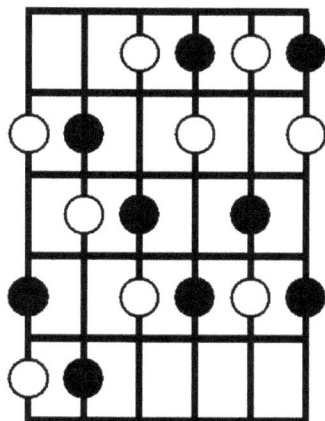

1.

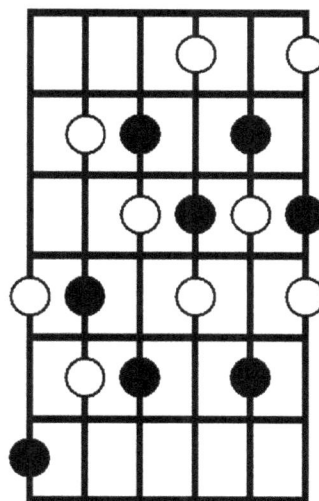

2.

3.

4.

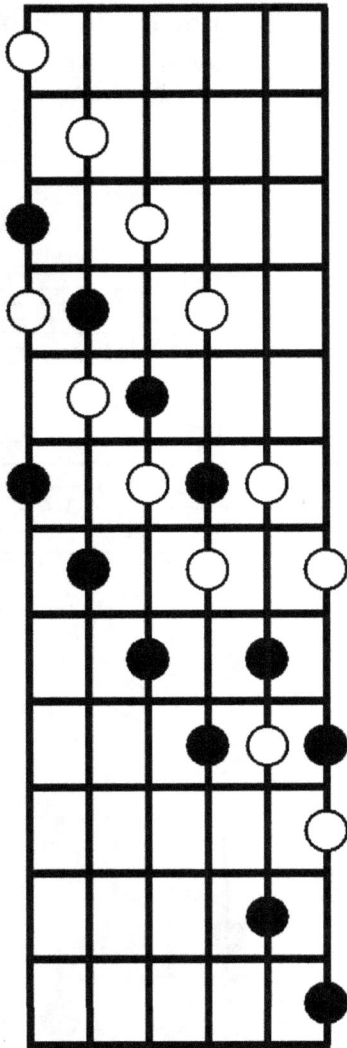

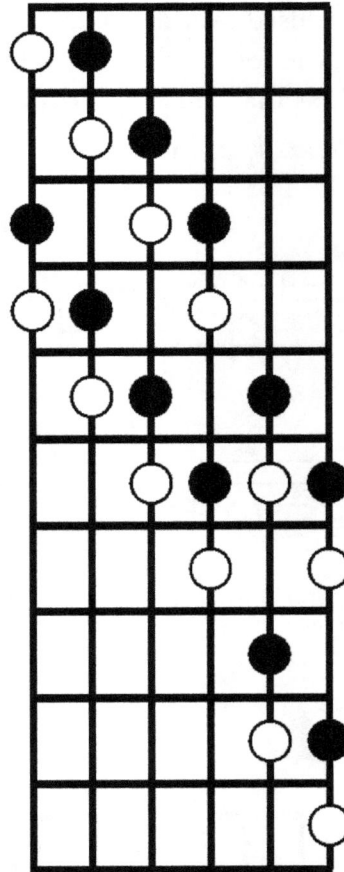

Every other note of a diminished scale can be considered to be a root note: for example, an A diminished scale contains the same notes as a C diminished scale. For this reason each scale shape has more than one root note marked.

Whole Tone Scale

The notes in a whole tone scale are all a whole tone apart. Because of this, every note in the scale shapes below can potentially be a tonic note (there are actually only two whole tone scales). Whole tone scales have a very characteristic sound, and can be used to play over dominant flat-five or sharp-five chords.

Scale spelling: 1, 2, 3, #4, #5, ♭7

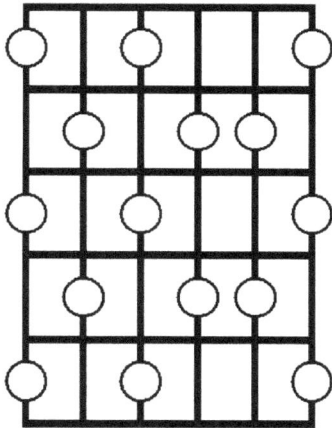

1.

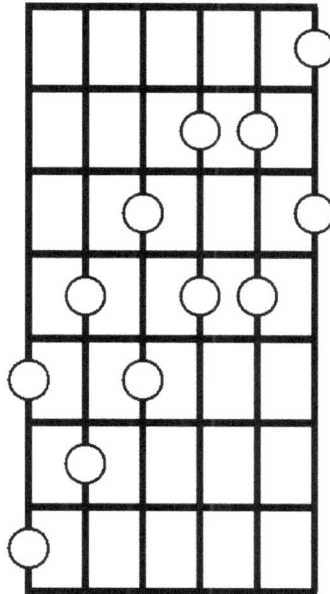

2.

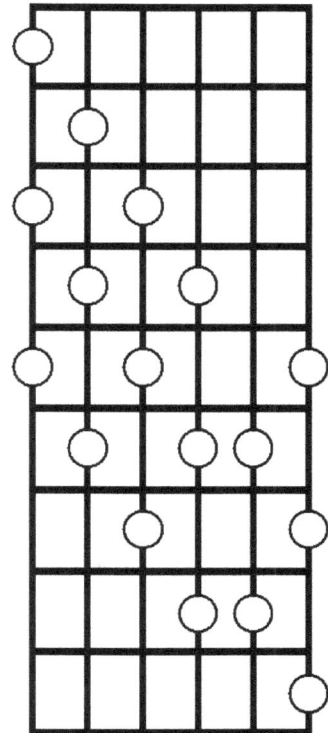

3.

Chromatic Scale

The chromatic scale moves in half-steps. Every note in chromatic scale shapes can be a tonic note. Playing chromatic scales is a good warm-up exercise.

1.

2.

Play this scale either by using your index finger to play the first two notes on each string apart from the second (B) string, OR by using your little finger to play the last two notes on each string apart from the second (B) string.

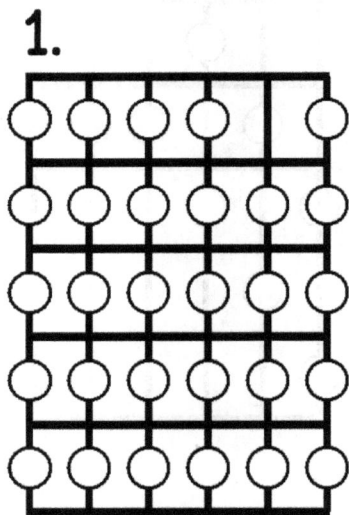

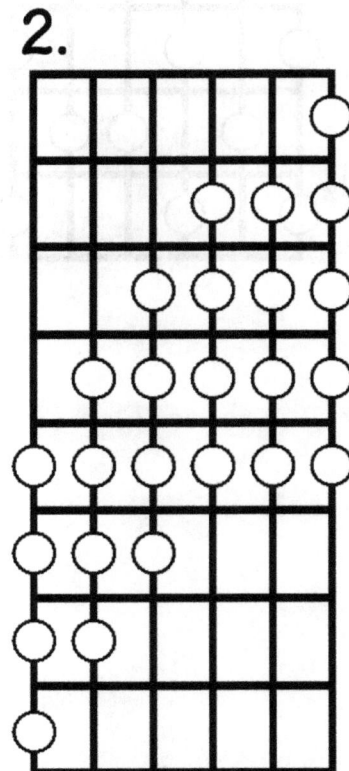

Japanese Scales

The following Japanese scales are all pentatonic (i.e. they are comprised of five notes). These scales are used in Japanese folk melodies and can be very inspiring to experiment with: use them to create atmospheric melodies or improvisations.

In Scale

Hirajoshi

Yo Scale

Scale Spellings For Japanese Pentatonic Scales:

In Scale: 1, ♭2, 4, 5, ♭6

Hirajoshi: 1, 2, ♭3, 5, ♭6

Yo Scale: 1, 2, 4, 5, 6

Arpeggios

Arpeggios are chords in which the notes are played one at a time, rather than all at once. All of the arpeggio diagrams in this section are 'movable' shapes, with the root notes being represented by the white circles.

Arpeggios can be used in improvisation and to create riffs and melodies.

Arpeggios Section 1

In this section 2-octave arpeggios are shown in tab and notation with a root of C. The diagrams show the arpeggios continuing upwards and downwards to include all of the potential notes for each position.

Arpeggios Section 2

The second section contains extended dominant and minor arpeggios. In this section the notation and diagrams show the full arpeggio, and are not extended below the root note or further extended above the highest note.

Arpeggios Section 1
Major

Minor

1. **2.** **3.** **4.** **5.**

Dominant 7th

1. **2.** **3.** **4.** **5.**

Minor 7th

Major 7th

Major Add 9

Minor Add 9

Diminished 7th

Minor 7th Flat 5

Arpeggios Section 2
Dominant 9th

Dominant 11th

Dominant 13th

Minor 9th

Minor 11th

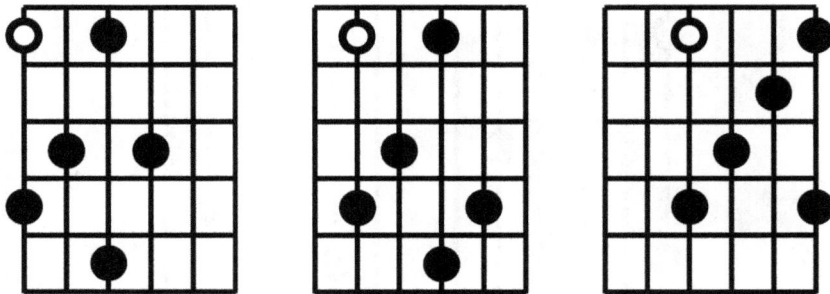

Minor 13th

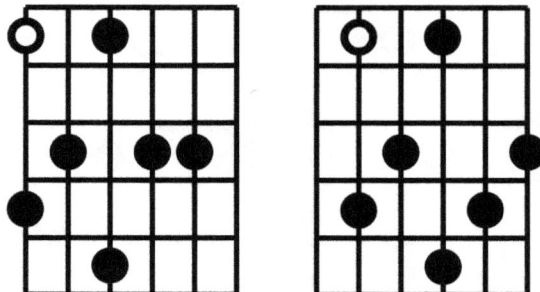

Guitar Command Backing Tracks

Improve Your Lead Guitar Playing With Scales And Modes

You're the lead guitarist.

After the second chorus you have 16 bars to make the song your own.

Is your guitar solo going to be dull, safe and uninspired, or is it going to be a memorable piece of music in its own right?

Break away from the crowd and go with option 2. Use your knowledge of the fretboard to create solos that your fans will love.

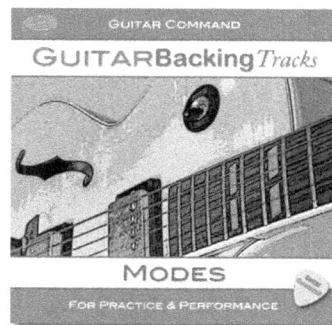

Download Guitar Command Backing Tracks from Amazon, iTunes, and many other stores.

Guitar Scales and **Guitar Modes** backing tracks albums have been specially produced for lead guitarists wishing to learn, and practice playing with, scales and modes.

Each track has been written to allow improvisation with a specific scale.

• Learn the scales and modes, then turn them into great music

• Master playing different scales all over the neck and add depth to your solos

Guitar Command Backing Tracks allow you to make the most of your practice time, giving you the advantage you need to stand out from the crowd.

Check out these other awesome backing tracks albums:

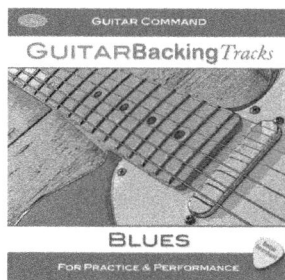

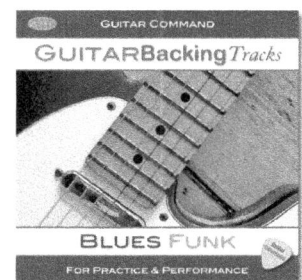

Make your solo the highlight of the song.

www.ingramcontent.com/pod-product-compliance
Lightning Source LLC
Chambersburg PA
CBHW062053090426

42740CB00016B/3112